JAPAN

— AN —

A-Z

A Guide to Living and Working in Japan

CATHERINE DEVRYE

HarperCollins*Publishers*

A percentage of the author's royalties from the sale of this book will be donated to The Sir Edward Dunlop Cancer Research Fellowship Fund of the Anti-Cancer Council of Victoria.

HarperCollins Publishers

25 Ryde Road, Pymble, Sydney NSW 2073, Australia
31 View Road, Glenfield, Auckland 10, New Zealand

First published in Australia in 1994

National Library of Australia
Cataloguing-in-Publication data:

DeVyre, Catherine.
    Japan: an A–Z: a guide to living and working in Japan.

    Includes index.
    ISBN 0 7322 5044 7.

    1. Business enterprises, Foreign—Japan—Handbooks, manuals, etc. 2. Negotiation in business—Japan—Handbooks, manuals, etc. 3. Business etiquette—Japan—Handbooks, manuals, etc. 4. Export marketing—Australia—Handbooks, manuals, etc. I. Title.

658.848

Cover illustration by Tony Pyrzakowski
Cover design by Darian Causby
Printed in Australia by Griffin Paperbacks, Adelaide

9 8 7 6 5 4 3 2 1
97 96 95 94

ACKNOWLEDGEMENTS

There is an old Japanese proverb: 'Hachiju no tenari', which translates as taking lessons in penmanship at the age of eighty. It can be roughly interpreted in one of two ways . . . that you can't teach an old dog new tricks or you're never too old to learn!

I would like to thank my outstanding team of Japanese staff for teaching an old dog valuable lessons. Until the day I die, I will never forget their competence, commitment, patience and friendship.

Domo arigato gozaimasu!

This book would not be complete without also expressing appreciation to:

♦ IBM for providing me with the opportunity, especially Ver Pena, Rod Puleo, Roy Lea and Jack Yellowleas;

♦ Kazu Tawa-san for his foreword and Lois and Russ Fynmore for introducing us. Also, John McKindley from Mitsui;

♦ my Japanese language teacher, practical adviser and friend, Miyoko Fukushima;

♦ *all* the wonderful people I met in Japan; Japanese and expatriates alike. I feel fortunate to reflect on those friends in Tokyo who were there to play sport, share a meal, head off to some unknown destination or share a moment of laughter. Thanks also to the colleagues from home who brought supplies of Aussie newspapers and chocolate and were always at the end of a telephone with an understanding ear.

♦ and, of course, Angelo Loukakis and the entire team at Harper Collins.

About the author

Catherine DeVrye spent two years in Tokyo as IBM's personnel manager for Asia Pacific Headquarters. In addition to general human resource issues, she was responsible for the housing, schooling and medical requirements of 600 expatriate families from over a dozen countries. With a very competent and almost exclusively Japanese staff, she managed a multimillion dollar budget.

She held various other marketing, communication and education positions with IBM in Australia and Hong Kong, before becoming CEO of Young Achievement Australia, and a member of the NSW Police Board.

Prior to joining IBM, she worked with a state government, responsible for funding to sporting organisations. She later served as a speech writer and press secretary to two government ministers.

She obtained a Bachelor of Physical Education degree from the University of Calgary and a Master of Science degree from the University of Montana. She subsequently attended short management courses conducted by Harvard University and Colgate Darden Management School.

She is a frequent broadcaster and author of numerous magazine and newspaper articles, and has previously published books on sports marketing and customer service.

The 1993 winner of the 'Telecom Australian Executive Woman of the Year' award.

Catherine has also been a university lecturer and visiting syndicate leader at the Australian Management

College, Mount Eliza. She gives frequent motivational presentations on customer service, change and leadership. Clients consist of leading business and government organisations such as the Australian Institute of Management, IBM, Mercedes-Benz, 3M, Royal Australian Navy and the World Triathlon Championships.

FOREWORD

BY KAZU TAWA

SENIOR ADVISER TO EXECUTIVE MANAGEMENT,
MITSUI MINING AND SMELTING CO. LTD, TOKYO.

KAZU TAWA

A female executive is still a rare species in Japan, giving this book a special quality at the outset.

Basing it on two years' experience as head of personnel at IBM Tokyo, Catherine wonders if this might be judged too short a time to present an expert view on Japan. In my opinion, she shows an acute observation and has used her time well. She has played the part of a 'voyeur' cleverly and correctly. Her book captures those fresh impressions prolonged exposure tends to dull, as I have myself experienced during six years in New York and a total of ten years in Australia over two assignments.

This serious, yet enjoyable, book is presented in the form of an A–Z guide. Catherine's recurrent theme, 'Treat each situation and individual uniquely', is convincingly argued. It is a message which I support and count as crucial to those who want to better understand people management in Japan, especially expatriates working in my country.

The reader will find that despite–or perhaps because of–modern media, some prior perceptions about the Japanese way of doing business are based on many myths. For example, Catherine downplays the notion that Japanese workers are reluctant to take time off. She notes that the number of public holidays is as great as that of Australia if not even greater.

The Japanese receptiveness to suggestions from workers and enterprise union systems are clearly shown to have benefits for both sides. Such evidence should find special interest in Australia where, whether influenced by Japan or not, some industries are clearly moving in these directions.

Catherine points out–fairly in my opinion–a worrying lack of opportunities for women in Japan. She sees this as just as much due to female shyness and a lamentable tendency to giggle as to male chauvinism. I share the belief that how much the former is due to the latter is a matter for debate.

Another focal point for discussion is the approach to recruitment in Japan. As Catherine found, business does to a large extent hire directly from favourite universities. Once recruited, employees are provided with ongoing in-house training which not only improves performance but nourishes abiding loyalty. As a graduate of this traditional practice, I wonder how it will be valued by future generations. Whatever the answer, there is undoubted value in Catherine's judgement that the success of Japan has been greatly assisted by a system with such strong emphasis on tertiary education.

On the lighter side, Catherine looks at the avid enthusiasm of Japanese for sporting events, particularly baseball, both on and off the playing field. Being an outstanding sportswoman in her own right, she has been able to gain unusual insights into what is an integral part of corporate life in Japan, along with the drinking and partying of company entertaining.

Her observations score highly with me. She has seen that in spite of the Japanese devotion to sports, actual participation in many activities–skiing for example–appears to run second to the visual impact of the outfit. Many of my fellow Japanese, the younger in particular, may care to disagree. But I regard it as a fair comment.

This book makes a truly valuable contribution to the subject of managing human resources in Japan. I trust all readers will find it as informative and entertaining as I do.

Contents

INTRODUCTION

After three months as personnel manager for a multinational company based in Tokyo, I thought I knew quite a bit about people management in Japan. After two years, I realised just how much I still had to learn! I never did learn enough to be the ideal manager but at least gained some insight from my mistakes and hope others may benefit from that knowledge.

This book will not provide answers to all your questions on doing business with Japan. It will probably be out of date by the time you read it because the environment is changing so quickly. But, it will give a broad overview of some unique practices. This should be useful if you or your organisation is typical of others which have done business in Japan.

Unlike other books on doing business with the Japanese, this one will not insult that nation by suggesting Westerners should treat all Japanese in the same manner. Certainly, Japan is a more homogeneous nation than most but it is still critical that one does not slip into a trap of gross overgeneralisation. Imagine the lack of credibility of books written on how to deal with the British suggesting all citizens of the United Kingdom be treated in identical fashion!

That is not to criticise other management books on Japan. Most of the information contained, in many excellent publications, was relevant in the 1980s. It served a useful purpose in the past. Depending on the particular text, a large percentage of the material is equally relevant today; and may well be so tomorrow. But, whatever you do as a reader, please do not accept this or any other information simply because it is printed in black and white.

Each situation must be viewed independently because people of all nationalities are unique. The identification, assessment and management of those unique traits must surely be the fundamental skill of successful business people.

Once you understand that Japanese workers do not look, think or act alike, you are moving towards an understanding of how to effectively manage in that country.

Do not take this, or any other publication, as gospel. There is no simple textbook solution to situations you will encounter. Gather your own information. Ask questions. Find a Japanese confidante with whom you can air situations by asking such questions as: 'I've heard that it is the practice to . . . Is that your experience in this company?'

Do not fall into the trap of believing that management is surrounded by mystique in Japan. When asking why a certain situation is so, do not simply accept the standard reply: 'Because it's the Japanese way', or 'Because things are different in Japan'.

By the way, the Japanese have helped create this mystique surrounding their organisations and culture. At times, they have openly argued they are different to protect their domestic markets. Some of those proposed differences, as cited by Pat Choate in the *Harvard Business*

Review, (October 1990: 102) are:

* In 1978, the Japanese government refused to permit imports of American-made blood analysers because, it asserted, the Japanese have 'different' blood.
* In 1986, foreign companies were not allowed to participate in the land reclamation work of the Kansai airport construction project because, the Japanese argued, they would have 'different' dirt.
* In 1986, MITI (the Ministry of International Trade and Industry) attempted to prevent US and European ski manufacturers from offering their products in Japan because Japan has 'different' snow.
* In 1987, US garbage disposals were kept out of the Japanese market because Japan has a 'different' sewerage system.
* In 1987, US beef imports to Japan were limited because the Japanese have intestines which are a 'different' length from other people's.
* In 1990, the Japanese tried to keep out US lumber exports, because the wood wouldn't withstand Japanese earthquakes, which are 'different' from those in the US. \

The word 'different' can be most frustrating if you merely accept this explanation. But, try using the 'D' word to your advantage. Ask questions of different people in different parts of the organisation. Then make a judgement about what is best by balancing traditional practice with the necessary requirements to be successful in the future.

A few years ago, Westerners readily accepted many of the economic myths surrounding the great industrial giant known as Japan. With the current recession and political upheaval which has dominated the press in recent times, outsiders are now separating myth from reality and recognising that there are not, and never have been, any magical solutions for business success in Japan . . . or any other nation.

Because Western companies have only competed with the most successful of Japanese companies, we know little of the failures; and it is easy to exaggerate management competence. Many unsuccessful Japanese organisations have the same personnel practices as the successful ones. So, once again, it is important to emphasise the need to assess each circumstance on its merits.

As more Westerners visit Japan, and increasing numbers of Japanese travel outside their island shores, the country is moving more to the forefront of the world stage; and the myths of unqualified success are rapidly evaporating. The nation, as a whole, is becoming more individualistic and not as set in traditional patterns of behaviour.

I shudder to think how little I knew when I first landed at Narita airport. In the first few months, the learning curve was so incredibly steep that I should, rightfully, have been equipped with the safety ropes of a mountaineer!

It took no time at all to discover that Japan isn't all cherry blossoms and picturesque views of Mount Fuji. In fact, one seldom sees Mount Fuji through the industrial haze. But, everywhere on the landscape, there are people; in fact 122 million of them. There are more residents in metropolitan Tokyo alone than all of Australia. So, it's not surprising that lasting impressions are not of *sumo* or *sushi*

4

but of the people; and that's why it is so important to understand human resource management in Japan.

There were times when I thought I would never understand. There were times when I didn't even want to try. In the course of writing this book, I re-read my diary and must confess surprise at one entry which read: 'Only 22 months and 11 days to go but who's counting'.

It wasn't always easy. There were times when I was desperately homesick. There were some foods I never got used to. There were days when I thought I couldn't bear being squashed in the subway one more time. There were friends I missed at home. And, mostly, I longed for the wide open spaces which I'd always taken for granted in Canada and Australia.

I begrudged paying more for two golf games than the cost of an annual membership in one of Australia's championship courses. Could I afford to live here if I needed to pay $90 for a melon? I wished my hairdresser could speak English. I reminisced about my five-minute walk to the beach at home as I sat in freeway traffic for two hours on my way back from the nearest beach in Tokyo.

Is this the same person whose diary entry two years later read: 'I wish I didn't need to leave Japan so soon'?

How did the time, which originally dragged, pass so quickly? Very simply, I changed *my* attitude. I no longer expected things to be like home. Nor did I expect to encounter situations described in textbooks. I learned simply to expect the unexpected and adapt accordingly.

After only two years, I was much more comfortable at Narita airport than at John F. Kennedy and it was always good to get 'home' to Tokyo after a business trip to New York.

I now look back on my time in Japan as one of the most rewarding in my working life. I am grateful to have had such a wonderful opportunity to gain first-hand experience with Australia's number one trading partner; to be involved in a culture that has brought true meaning to the term Pacific Rim, at a time when the United States sees more trade flowing across the Pacific than the Atlantic.

I may be arrogant to believe I now know more than most other Western executives about management in Japan. Yet, I must be correspondingly humble to admit I probably know only a fraction of what even the average shop floor worker in Japan *really* comprehends about the realities of management in their country.

Although I am supposedly familiar with Japanese hiring processes, I encountered a particular situation which was foreign to me whilst writing this book. On being asked whether I would be available to lunch with executives of a Japanese firm operating in Australia, I eventually realised I was being head-hunted. I had no experience of head-hunting in Japan, and had read in other books that head-hunting was not done; even less likely of females, and certainly not over lunch. It was a situation where I could draw on my own advice: *Treat each situation and individual uniquely!*

Japan is changing. These changes are not and will not occur overnight. They are, in fact, happening to greater degrees in certain segments of the economy and different geographic pockets. It could be safely said that metropolitan Tokyo is much more Westernised than a small town in the northern island of Hokkaido. Yet, that is not to say that some residents of a small village may not be more Westernised and cosmopolitan in their outlook than someone else in downtown Tokyo. Again, it is dangerous to overgeneralise.

Just like Western companies, practices also vary between industries, according to the personalities of departmental heads and so on. You will be surprised at how many similarities there are with the challenges currently confronting Western human resource management, issues such as smoking for which no one has a universally accepted workplace solution.

Let's face it—in today's global economy, it isn't easy doing business anywhere in the world. Akio Morita, chairman of Sony, sums it up in his book *Made in Japan:*

> 'Many foreigners complain how difficult it is to do business in Japan but when in America for the first time, I felt it would be impossible to do well in that enormous market'. (p. 293)

So don't be worried if you don't understand everything about doing business in Japan. You probably never will. But, it is better to know what you do not know than think you understand what you really do not!

This book will open the kimono a little and dispel some myths. It will provide an A to Z glimpse of some things which may be applicable to the operations of your company in Japan.

Don't worry about trying to absorb a lot of information now, and then, many months later, attempt to recall what was said about a certain situation. The alphabetical format is such that you can use this book as an easy reference guide if, and when, a situation arises. Some entries are long. Some are short. All contain cross references to related entries.

And, after you've had the opportunity to personally experience business dealings with the Japanese, you'll no doubt be able to add comments of your own because if I've said it once, I'll say it a thousand times, 'Each individual and situation is unique'.

A

ACCOMMODATION

Japan is a very mountainous country and only a third of the land is suitable for human occupation. With available space at such a premium, real estate prices are extremely high. A square inch of real estate is worth US$151! This works out to about US$14 000 for a piece of land the size of an A4 page. To give a comparison, a square inch of land in midtown Manhattan averages $12.50.

A *tsubo* is the normal measure of land area. It is a spot of land of 3.3 square metres and can be worth over 100 million yen (about one million Australian dollars). This makes it virtually impossible for the average young couple to buy a home. With such prices, their dream of home ownership becomes a nightmare and it is easy to see why many choose to spend their income on overseas travel, as there is little point saving to buy a home of one's own.

Even a nearby parking space can sell for a staggering US$130 000. It is estimated that land surrounding Tokyo and Yokohama is now worth more than the entire United States.

Finding a place to live in a strange city is always a challenge. It becomes more so if you don't speak the language, but fortunately, most major real estate companies in Tokyo have English-speaking staff. They will pick you up from your hotel and show you a range of accommodation. You will be impressed with their politeness but remember, they are no different from realtors anywhere else in the world. Their objective is to get the best price so make sure you have an idea of your requirements and approximate price range. Talk to at least a couple of agents and invest the time to see a few properties before choosing.

As charming as these realtors are, realise that 'buyer/renter beware' still applies. I realised this very early when I said *Domo* (thank you) to one agent, who then insisted I spoke very good Japanese in spite of my assurances it was, in fact, the only word in my vocabulary at the time!

Through no choice of my own, I became a bit of an authority on housing in Tokyo. Part of my responsibilities as Headquarters personnel manager included managing the accommodation requirements of 600 expatriate families. Because IBM chose to provide housing allowances separate from the salary package, the expense was phenomenal. In fact, it exceeded the pre-tax operating profit of many smaller IBM operations in other countries.

With a huge influx of expatriates and initial shortages of Western accommodation, realtors fully recognised the law of supply and demand. IBM was accused of pushing up rental prices in Tokyo in 1985. This was to some extent true, but likewise, there was an increase in the number of other foreign companies moving to Tokyo at the time. What I found amusing was that a couple of years later, IBM was again being accused by realtors in the press as being responsible for the downturn in the housing market. The developers had built more apartments to cope with the demand and now there didn't seem to be the same number of foreigners moving to Tokyo. Therefore, it was IBM's 'fault' these developers were 'losing' money by necessarily charging lower rents because supply had exceeded demand.

This economic reality is a good reason why one should shop comparatively before choosing an apartment as the rentals may vary considerably, even over a period of a few months. As is common practice in Western countries, a security bond (key money) and advance rent is required.

With all the confusion surrounding a move to a new country, you'll find you can easily be confused after looking at a number of places. To help overcome this, I typed my essential criteria on a sheet of paper and then made numerous photocopies. That provided an easy reference point before deciding on an apartment (which turned out to be the second one I saw after looking at over a dozen).

The following list can be modified easily. For example, those with children would want to be located near a school, or transport to a school. Each individual has unique preferences but it must be remembered that downtown Tokyo can *not* provide the same amenities that one may be used to in a beach suburb of Sydney or acreage on the outskirts of Silicon Valley.

And, if you wish to purchase a car, you must first be able to prove you have a place to keep it.

Refer also to: Business cards

CHECK LIST

DATE ....

AGENT ....

ADDRESS...

COST ....

TERMS ....

LOCATION...

TRANSPORT

QUIET

PARKING AVAILABLE

SECURITY

BEDROOMS . . .
NUMBER
BUILT-INS
POWER-POINTS

KITCHEN . . .
DISHWASHER
SHELVES
STORAGE
STOVE
OVEN
TILES
POWER-POINTS
LIGHTING

LIVING . . .
DINING-AREA
LOUNGE SIZE

LAUNDRY AREA . . .

BATHROOM . . .
TOILET
SHOWER
BATHBASIN
VANITY
WATER PRESSURE
TILES
POWER-POINTS
COLOUR

STORAGE

HEATING

COOLING SCREENS

LIGHT . . .
NATURAL
FITTINGS

CARPET/FLOOR COVERINGS

WINDOW COVERINGS

(FEW DWELLINGS HAVE)

OTHER COMMENTS (E.G. CRACKS IN WALL) ....
....
....
....

ALLOWANCES AND BENEFITS

Salaries, because still largely based on age and seniority, are much the same between first and fourth line managers. However, allowances and benefits are notably different. The more senior employees may receive a car, complete with driver and feather duster; a maid; a million dollar golf club membership or access to other recreational facilities.

Because the average commuting time is one and a half hours by train each way, it is not uncommon for late-working employees to be accommodated in a hotel with a meal allowance. Companies may also provide a commuting allowance, housing loan allowance, insurance and family allowance. The amounts vary widely.

Employees may have access to group travel schemes, recreation facilities and company-owned vacation resorts. These are very popular so the allocation is often done on a lottery basis to ensure fairness.

Refer also to: Bonus, Hygiene factors, Lifelong employment, Salary, Sport and recreation, Unions

AUTOMOBILES

With horrendous traffic jams in Tokyo, one would seriously question the advantage of purchasing an automobile to risk life and limb driving in an environment where you understand none of the language on the road signs! However, many expatriates successfully and enjoyably manoeuvre a car around Japan on the left-hand side of the road.

In order to purchase a car, you must first prove you have access to off-street parking. The dealer will obtain, from the police, the necessary garage certificate for a fee of about 5000 yen, which verifies you have such a spot. The dealer will also arrange licence plates and registration. You simply need to provide a certificate from your embassy with your signature.

Third party insurance is compulsory. Again, the dealer will arrange this for you. It is renewable every two years. Optional personal property insurance is recommended and available from a wide range of internationally known names in insurance provision.

Automobile taxes are payable and if you wish to import a car from overseas, stringent requirements apply which should be checked with the Japanese consulate in your home country, prior to departure.

After purchasing a new car, an inspection is necessary three years from the date of purchase and every two years thereafter. A sticker is placed on the windscreen and no reminder is sent, so make careful note of the date. The inspection can be as costly as 150 000 yen.

To obtain a Japanese driver's licence, you will need a current licence from your own country, passport, alien registration card and two black and white photographs (3.5 cm X 2.5 cm). You will be required to take an eye examination. The licence will expire on your birthday three years after you obtain it. No reminders are sent, so the onus is on you to renew.

If you do not have a driver's licence from your own country, you will need to sit a very difficult test, including questions on engine operations and repairs!

Rules of the road are available from the Japanese Automobile Federation and heavy penalties are applied for infringements.

Refer also to: Baggage, Transport, Visas and other legal documents

B

BAGGAGE

Air travellers need no written declaration for accompanying baggage and effects cleared through customs at the time of arrival. For travellers arriving by sea, a declaration must be made in writing to cover accompanied and unaccompanied baggage.

Unaccompanied baggage must arrive within six months of entry to Japan. A form must be filled out in duplicate and verified by customs at the port of entry. Pets must also be declared on this form as well as an automobile, if you chose to ship one.

Record as much detail as you can and be sure to keep one copy! There is a great deal of bureaucracy involved in this procedure and if you don't strictly adhere to the rules, it can make your arrival in Japan very unpleasant.

Unused household appliances are subject to duty.

Foreigners coming to Japan may bring in duty-free liquor, perfume, tobacco and jewellery to a certain value. It is best to check the allocations prior to purchase.

Importation of live and raw products is prohibited.

There is no restriction on the amount of money which may be brought into the country and foreign currency may be readily exchanged for yen.

Refer also to: Automobiles, Banking, Pets, Shopping, Visas

BANKING

There are over 60 foreign banks in Japan, as well as the popular post office savings accounts, used extensively by the average worker.

Renowned as a cash society, Japan is making a rapid transition towards credit, spurred by a youthful and affluent populace. Cash is still the preferred medium for transactions. Cheques remain unpopular, no doubt due to a government regulation that if an overdraft is not paid by 3.00 p.m. on the day the cheque is presented, a customer loses all credit privileges for a minimum of two years and often a lifetime, eliminating even a minimal margin of error for an honest mistake.

Like most other businesses in Japan, the focus in banking is on service and starts with wooing the top university graduates to a lifetime career. When entering a Japanese bank, there appear to be at least two of these highly qualified staff for every customer. Yet, to a Westerner, the service still seems slow, especially with foreign transactions. This is due to meticulous checking of records but one ponders if it could possibly relate to decisions as to what type of gift a customer should receive upon depositing a sum of money.

Although specialised firms are responsible for the 'scientific selection' of these gifts, the choice of such presents as tissues, toilet paper, tin foil, towels and bandaids remain a mystery to the Western mind.

Most Westerners would prefer higher interest rates, which are regulated by the government. These are uniformly low for all banks, which has led to relatively recent marketing and advertising drives to attract and retain customers through other means.

Utility bills, television charges and taxes may be paid by automatic deduction, and electronic tellers have become common in recent years. These come complete with a computerised graphics screen of a bowing female teller and a pleasant voice overture thanking you for your business.

You may withdraw funds from any bank in Japan, including the automatic tellers of the competitive banks for a nominal fee. Losing face is unacceptable in Japanese society so the government, with yet another of its many regulations, protects the banks from such a fate by decreeing automatic tellers only remain open (and staffed!) between 8.45 a.m. and 7.00 p.m. on weekdays. Many banks and automatic teller machines are also open on Saturday mornings.

Magnifying glasses and an array of spectacles are provided for those with poor sight to fill in the forms. The lobby contains magazines to read while you wait.

As many banks are part of huge conglomerates, they have affiliations with travel agents, sports clubs, health insurance plans, and publish booklets on real estate, law and other issues of consumer interest.

Banks do more than dispense and receive money. A branch may help a business locate office space, lease computers and, more importantly, act as a go-between to introduce a foreign company to potential important contacts.

Those making application for a loan should be personally introduced to the bank manager, preferably by someone willing to act as a guarantor.

Refer also to: Discretion . . . loss of face, Service

BASEBALL

Although the entry on sport covers a wide range of recreational activities, baseball is in a category of its own. Believe it or not, it does, in fact, have implications for management. Let me explain . . .

Industrial leagues are very popular and the reputation of a company can be enhanced by the success of its baseball team. Leagues are semiprofessional and some employees are actually recruited solely for their athletic abilities.

So, what, you may ask, does this have to do with management? Depending on their work skills, these players are allocated jobs in the company which would be expected to occupy only part of their time, with the remainder of the working day reserved for practice. The personnel department is expected to be very understanding of the priorities between working and winning.

If a team should be fortunate to make the finals, it would not be at all unusual for thousands of employees to attend the game; and receive time off from their jobs to do so! The company may even charter a train or bus. There are cheer squads and enthusiastic support from the chairman down.

When I lived in Japan, the IBM team from our manufacturing plant in the town of Yasu (about 300 kilometres from Tokyo) qualified for the national semifinals. A bullet train was chartered to Tokyo and the mayor of the locality travelled with the contingent to support the IBM 'home' team. Twenty thousand workers attended during office hours, including the president. A video was made to show all those who couldn't attend; and this was later used for motivational talks in the various sections. Every employee also received a five-page description of the game . . . and we didn't even win!

A number of people in our personnel department were affiliated with the team to ensure their welfare was adequately catered for, as well as the logistics and safety concerns of transporting such a large number of fans. Presumably, there was also due consideration given to the impact on productivity and adequate staffing levels, with so many workers absent from the plant.

Interdepartmental games within companies are also common—with the expressed purpose of building team harmony. In theory, everyone is encouraged to participate but the reality is that the most athletic usually take the field with the lesser skilled assigned to roles as cheerleaders, bat boys etc. Everyone seems to enjoy these afternoons and the associated socialising afterward.

About three months after arriving in Japan, there was a softball game between our section and another department. Our team lost but I'm quite convinced that my status in the organisation was significantly raised as a result of receiving the 'Golden Glove' award for the most valuable player on our side. It seemed that my mis-spent youth on the parking lots of Canada had finally paid dividends! This may sound somewhat tongue in cheek but both my boss and I did sense a certain difference in the office after that game; possibly because any form of even mediocre athletic performance is not at all expected of a female!

If I'd had any premonition of the significance of this social game, I would probably have paid a visit to a baseball practice range. This is similar to a golf driving range whereby you pay a sum of money which entitles you to hit a set number of balls pitched from an automatic machine. You select your bat and nominate speeds of 80 or 100 kilometres per hour, while balls are projected as you stand in a batting net.

Refer also to: Sport and recreation, Vacations

BONUS

Approximately one-third of annual compensation is paid on a semi-annual basis. In other words, every June and December, employees usually receive a bonus of three to four months' salary. This allows companies not only to have the use of the funds until the bonus is paid but also to control salaries. If business is poor, there is no bonus or a reduced amount. In tough economic times, employees do not receive a salary cut—just a reduced bonus. This has the additional benefit for employees of reducing the likelihood of lay-offs. The other advantage to the company is that the bonus is non-pensionable income so is not taken into account when calculating severance or retirement pay.

The basic premise of the bonus system is that all members share in the success or failure of the company, but the reality today is that the bonus has become an expectation of all employees. Reductions and rises in bonuses are directly related to productivity and affect all employees proportionately. Executives and shop-floor assistants, alike, all stand to benefit by working toward a profitable result for the company. There is usually a 30–40 per cent range which allows a firm to give more compensation to those employees who have performed best during that year.

In certain instances, consumer companies may offer products as part of a year-end bonus to clear supply. This would usually not be regarded as favourably as cash; and if the supply of available goods is less than the number of eligible employees, a lottery may be held to determine who wins the products. When IBM Japan celebrated its 50th anniversary, they had a surplus of personal computers but only enough to distribute to two-thirds of the work force. The other third were compensated with special coffee cups designed for the occasion . . . hardly an equitable reward. I was amazed that although there was obvious disappointment among some, there were no signs of staff discontent, because the lottery system of distribution was seen as fair.

Bonuses are also paid to domestic staff (maids, gardeners, drivers), which means you should calculate the equivalent of 20 months salary for 12 months of actual work. I initially found it a rather appalling system when digging into my pocket to pay my maid the bonus, until I realised that this was the norm and their monthly salary adjusted downward accordingly to make allowances for the bonus system. It came as an initial shock to my personal finances but I soon accepted it as routine and it certainly eliminated any question of what one should or shouldn't give staff in terms of bonuses or Christmas gifts.

The bonus system is probably the key reason why Japan has the highest savings rate in the world, because it is estimated that approximately half of all bonuses are assiduously saved every year.

Refer also to: Allowances and benefits, Gift giving, Lifelong employment, Obligation, Salary

BOWING

There have been entire books devoted to bowing and business cards. I will not attempt to delve into all the intricacies of whether one should bow at a 45 or 90 degree angle, but will simply cover the basic things one needs to know about these topics.

Foreigners are not usually expected to bow. However, you should follow the lead of your Japanese counterpart. If your Japanese host bows, you will probably want to offer a similar bow. If they extend their hand, do likewise. These days, Japanese usually prefer to shake hands with Westerners but don't judge an individual as a wimp if the grasp is somewhat weaker than you would expect in the West. Remember, it's a different culture and most Japanese are no more familiar with the proper pressure to be applied to a handshake than Westerners are with the nuances of the appropriate bow.

Generally speaking, the deeper the angle of the bow the more respect one offers to the opposite party. There seem to be infinite variations on the appropriate degree of the angle of the bow, the number of times one should bow, the length of time spent in the bent position, where the hands should be placed etc. However, in this day and age, it is unusual that Westerners would be expected to adhere to the strict etiquette of bowing behaviour.

One may hear the odd story of seemingly endless bowing whereby each party tries to 'outbow' the other to indicate respect, because no one wants to be the first to stop. The best course of action is simply to follow the lead of the other party as to whether the greeting is a handshake or a bow. If it is the former, I would usually offer a small bow as well. If it is the latter, I would bow at approximately the same angle as the person I was meeting—but only once. I believe it is important to feel as natural and warm as possible when being introduced. It is difficult for your genuine personality to shine through if you are in an uncomfortable position for any length of time.

Refer also to: Communication . . . and useful phrases

BUSINESS CARDS

The key thing to remember is never (I repeat *never*) be without a business card. You would do well to adopt the American Express slogan: 'Don't leave home without it!' A business card (*meishi*) is essential to do business in Japan. It should have your name, title, address, phone number, fax number etc. It should be printed in English on one side and in Japanese on the other. It is extremely important that your title is carefully translated because your business card provides associates with an immediate indication of the appropriate status with which you should be regarded.

The card should be printed on high quality paper and only presented to someone if it is in pristine condition. Immediately dispose of any with ragged edges or smudge marks. You know the ones I mean . . . the accumulated collection in your wallet which have deteriorated over time or got mixed up with ones which have been presented to you. I would suggest you actually carry business cards in a separate holder, preferably a prestigious leather one as some counterparts will judge not only your card but the overall presentation. There may also be inadequate space in your wallet for the large number of business cards you should always have on hand.

It's always wise to carry twice as many as you expect to hand out in case the person you are meeting brings associates along. It would be expected that you would exchange cards with everyone present. You should not exchange business cards with people you have already met as it implies that you have forgotten them.

Present your card with the Japanese print face up and facing the receiver so it can be easily read at a glance. Hand and accept cards with both hands. Always carefully study and acknowledge the importance of the card of the person who is presenting you with their credentials. Nod and smile before carefully putting it away. Don't put it in your back pocket as it is considered an insult to sit on someone's identity! It is also inappropriate to write on another's *meishi*. Doing so is tantamount to scrawling on the very face of the provider.

With business cards printed on both sides, you are unable to use them for speech notes at the various speeches you will inevitably be asked to give! So, if you're like me and need a few key points scribbled down unobtrusively on the back of a small card which can be held neatly in the palm of your hand, bring those leftover cards from home for that purpose.

In addition to business cards, many Westerners living in Japan also have 'home cards' printed. These contain your name, address and phone number in Japanese and your native language. The back of the card consists of a map depicting the immediate neighbourhood where you live, with major landmarks highlighted. As street addresses may be rather confusing for even the most dedicated taxi driver to logically decipher (there is no continuous numbering system or street naming), 'home cards' can save a great deal of frustration. They are also useful for home deliveries of any sort if handed to the proprietor at the time of purchase.

Refer also to: Communication . . . and useful phrases, Discretion . . . and loss of face, Names, Obligation

C

COMMUNICATION . . . AND USEFUL PHRASES

Sound communication is essential for effective management in any country. Whether it be formal business communication or interpersonal relationships, it is important to understand how to communicate a clear message and avoid the likelihood of misinterpretation which may result from insensitivity to a particular culture.

INTERPERSONAL COMMUNICATION

The basics of successful interpersonal communication are not always easy, given the language differences. If you are not fluent in Japanese, the most important thing to remember is to be patient and speak slowly and calmly at all times. Never resort to raising your voice or using pidgin English.

The best advice comes from my seventh grade teacher who wrote in my autograph book: 'Smiles are passports through deserts, and visas to all alien countries'.

I had no idea what a passport even was at the time but nearly a quarter of a century later, I learned that a sincere smile, coupled with elementary charades, could successfully manoeuvre me through most situations. I'll cover other aspects of non-verbal communication later but a smile is such a universal means of positive communication, it bears mentioning more than once.

Some of my fondest memories of communication in Japan were when I didn't speak a word of the language except *domo* (thank you). It was at times when I was totally lost and helpless that people came to my aid. Sometimes they wanted to practise their English while giving me directions or physically going out of their way to take me to my destination. But, at other times, not a single word was exchanged. I can still recall the kindness on an old man's face who handed me a pre-loved, hand-painted fan on a hot summer's day, apparently for the privilege of letting him take my picture. More often, I remember the smiles of children as I photographed them playing on the pavement.

Much to my surprise, I discovered that many younger Japanese had some knowledge of English and other foreign languages. However, their expertise may be more evident in the written than spoken form. This is because they are often taught English at school but due to large class sizes seldom have the opportunity to practise speaking and may be reluctant to do so for fear of embarrassment.

On the other hand, many welcome the opportunity to practise their English on a foreigner and this is one reason why people go out of their way to help a stranded tourist on a street corner.

It's really no different than a Western Canadian child like me, who learned French in school but never spoke it because Ukrainian was a more common language in our province. I can still read and comprehend a bilingual breakfast cereal package to this day, but in no way can make myself understood in a Parisian restaurant.

Of course, the best way to improve communications in Japan (or any other country for that matter) is to invest the necessary time to learn the language. The problem is that time seems to be at a premium, but it is still worthwhile to learn a few phrases.

You can listen to language tapes, enrol in a class, or have individual tuition. There are pros and cons to each of these methods. Audio tapes are the least expensive and can be used at your own pace but they obviously don't provide the opportunity to practise the language and receive feedback on pronunciation.

Language classes with other foreigners will provide this opportunity and also enable you to meet others who are experiencing similar difficulties to yourself. However, you must make yourself available for a regular commitment so you don't fall behind the class; and it can be equally frustrating if the rest of the class are slower learners than you.

Another option is to engage the services of a private tutor (*sensei*). This is the most expensive option but provides individual instruction, two-way conversation and also the opportunity to be taught specific phrases which you can use in your work. This is preferable to simply adhering to the rote learning contained in a text which may be of little use in the office. I benefited greatly from individual tuition because I wanted to immediately learn such business phrases as 'Keep up the good work'.

This was definitely preferable to routinely following a method of tuition which dictated I couldn't progress to the next section until I learned how to say 'May I have the ashtray please?'. As a non-smoker, this was totally useless to me, as was my original teacher who wouldn't provide the flexibility for me to learn what I wanted to. She also insisted that we only spoke Japanese during the lesson and although I appreciate the theory behind that immersion method, it didn't allow me to acquire information which I wanted to apply practically.

The second *sensei* I engaged understood my needs and not only provided me with the basic language skills, but became a good friend and imparted a wealth of knowledge about the culture and country. I was also able to use her as a confidante to ask about confusing personnel situations which arose in the office. She visited me in Australia recently and was appalled at how much of the language I had forgotten through disuse, but fortunately the friendship is still as strong as ever.

Admittedly, the best way to learn Japanese is to undertake an intensive immersion course and live with a non-English speaking family; particularly in a remote country area where you would be forced to understand the language to survive. However, this is usually not practical for the business person. If you do opt for such a learning environment, you should also be prepared to spend as much time teaching English as learning Japanese.

Although I firmly believe everyone should learn a few phrases to demonstrate you are at least trying to adapt, there is the risk that 'a little knowledge can be a dangerous thing'. In all likelihood, you could get a lengthy reply in Japanese to a few well chosen words, on the assumption that you must speak the language fluently. This is especially true when you are invisible in a telephone conversation and answer '*Moshi, moshi*' in the traditional greeting. The party at the other end has no idea that these words may represent the sum total of your vocabulary; and may proceed to launch into a lengthy dialogue, of which you don't understand a word. Still, I emphasise it is well worth the effort to learn a few phrases.

It's also important to take the opportunity to practise what you learn, even though you will inevitably make mistakes. I didn't have half as much knowledge as a couple of my friends but always seemed to be the spokesperson because they were too embarrassed to make mistakes. I've always been a firm believer that one who makes no mistakes, makes no progress. So, I was not at all hesitant to frequently make a fool of myself; but always managed to eventually communicate.

One classic example was my first weekend trip. On my return to Tokyo, I became very frustrated when the stationmaster couldn't seem to understand my simple question: 'What time does the train leave for Tokyo?' *Densha* is the word for train, *denwa* is the word for telephone, so we were both getting frustrated as I repeatedly asked him what time the *telephone* left for Tokyo . . . until I double-checked my dictionary.

Speaking of trains, I was always concerned about the bilingual announcements on the bullet trains, each time a station was approached. The Japanese message seemed very detailed and lasted a number of minutes. The English translation simply consisted of 'We will soon arrive at such and such destination'. I always wondered what they *weren't* telling me but it never seemed to be a problem as I always managed to get off at the correct stop.

Naturally, innocent misunderstandings go both ways. For example, how do you explain, to a non-English speaker, the phrase 'raining cats and dogs', or that shortbread is not really bread at all! Is it little wonder that many of the modern hotels had Japanese instructions on how to use a Western toilet!

On one occasion, I was climbing Mount Fuji and met a man who appeared to have a fun run advertised on his tee shirt. As we walked together, I asked in broken Japanese whether he jogged every morning. He responded in broken English that he did so three times a week. The conversation continued slowly in this vein with each of us trying to use the other's language to reply. All was progressing smoothly until I asked, 'Do you also run marathons?'

He looked puzzled so I explained the term marathon to the best of my ability in limited Japanese . . . 'It is very difficult and a very long time.'

'Oh yes,' he replied. 'Me marathon . . . and four children . . . very long time, very difficult!'

But don't let stories like this deter you from trying to use the language. The Japanese are very gracious and appreciate any effort which is made. Here are a few everyday phrases to get you started:

Thank you	*Domo*
Thank you very much	*Domo arigato*
Thank you very much (formal)	*Domo arigato gozaimasu*

Good morning	*Ohayo gozaimasu*
Hello	*Konnichi wa*
Please	*Dozo*
Sorry	*Gomennasai*
Excuse me please	*Sumimasen*
How are you	*O genki desu ka*
English	*Eigo*
Cheers	*Kampai*
Good-bye	*Sayonara*
Yes	*Hai*
No	!?!

'*Iie*' is the actual word for 'no' but it is *not* worth learning because it is a word seldom used and there are too many dangers in using it incorrectly.

I would strongly recommend that you only learn positive words to avoid any potentially insulting remarks. Rather than saying 'no', Japanese will simply keep quiet; or become vague; or answer with such euphemisms as: 'Very difficult', 'I'll check and see what I can do', 'I agree in principle but . . . I'm not sure'.

If an employee tells you that a request you have made is 'very difficult', it probably means they have no intention of even attempting it, but do not wish to offend you by saying a direct no. They are also likely to simply shake their head or suck air through their teeth; or simply stare blankly into space.

It is also critical to remember that 'yes' does not mean yes in Japan. It only implies that the person has understood your question or at least acknowledges that you have asked a question. For example, if you ask 'Is the meeting on the second floor', the answer is likely to be yes. You are likely to also receive a 'yes' if you say 'Where is the meeting?'

So, it is important to ask questions which can *not* be easily answered with a 'yes'. This will allow you to clarify understanding and it is a good idea to request a person to paraphrase your question to test for understanding.

Do not be surprised if you find people somewhat reluctant to ask direct questions for clarification. This may be because of embarrassment at their English skills or simply awkwardness because they feel they should know the answer. However, it may also be a sign of respect to you because asking a question could imply the manager or teacher did not adequately communicate and they would not want you to lose face.

Just as Westerners routinely say 'It was a pleasure to meet you', whether it was or not, don't read too much into the literal meaning of what Japanese may say. Like our own culture, there are some phrases which are said purely for the sake of etiquette. For example, if a Japanese person says 'Please drop by anytime' . . . don't.

Experts will tell you that the best approach is to keep communications simple in any language. This is particularly true when more than one language is involved, but is often easier said than done.

Do not believe that the Japanese are solemn and have no sense of humour. They enjoy laughter as much as we do. However, in any foreign culture, be careful that your humour is not open to misinterpretation. The safest bet is to tell only jokes which make fun of yourself or your own country.

Be careful with humour. Laughing with someone may

be incorrectly interpreted as laughing at them. Jokes may often fall flat because of nuances in language, but that is not to imply that every situation should be deadly serious. Quite the contrary . . . genuine humour and having fun can help create a more relaxed atmosphere; especially if poking fun at yourself.

It was always a good party trick to overhear conversations in Japanese, which were obviously concerning you. I got to the stage where I could usually understand enough to smile and say 'I'm just a crazy foreigner' . . . which would always bring a deluge of embarrassed giggles.

Remember that humour is universal although not every culture laughs at the same things. I used to find it a constant source of amusement whenever I saw a Japanese bowing on the other end of a telephone line. This seemed a particular quirk until one day I noticed a New Yorker wildly gesticulating with his hands in a phone booth. There was no difference! I never did quite get used to 'Home on the Range' as the standard background music while waiting on a call.

Most Japanese still tend to be very modest in their communications and are not generally as assertive as the average Westerner. You should therefore be careful not to appear boastful by apparently innocuous comments such as 'I have a nice swimming pool in my home' or 'My son does very well at school'. Although these may appear a simple statement of fact, it may be misconstrued as arrogant and designed to make the other person feel somewhat inferior.

By the same token, some Japanese may downplay their own importance by such statements as 'I am not sure if I can do it, but I will try' or 'I am only president of a small company' (when, in fact, there may be millions of dollars of turnover).

That is not to say that you will not encounter the person who grossly exaggerates their own importance. Try not to engage in one-upmanship which is often the norm in Western culture. If complimented, it is usually best to politely downplay it, which is quite contrary to current Western etiquette which says one should accept compliments gracefully.

There are also differences in non-verbal communication. As crowded as Tokyo trains are, the Japanese generally prefer more space between each other in a business setting. If a Japanese colleague steps back as you're talking, don't be offended that your deodorant didn't stand up to the subway rush hour. Resist the temptation to move progressively forward if they retreat. The extra distance is more comfortable by their standards.

Likewise, be more restrained in touching people. An ordinary pat on the back or touch on shoulder is not common and may be seen as an invasion of privacy.

Even facial expressions should be kept to a minimum. That means no wincing, gritting of teeth or looking skyward in disgust.

The importance of smiling has already been mentioned. That advice stands true but you should also be aware that a Japanese smile does not always signify pleasure. While attending the peace ceremony at Hiroshima, I was approached by an elderly woman who beamed a smile and said 'My son died over there'.

Why was she smiling when I was holding back tears? I later learned that a Japanese smile does not always indicate happiness but can be used as a mask to cover a wide array of emotions. However, in the majority of instances, it is safe to assume that a smile does, in fact, symbolise joy. It's a good test to notice if the eyes are also smiling . . . like the proverbial Irish song.

You will have the opportunity to meet Irish and every other nationality while living in Tokyo. My boss was a delightful expatriate with a unique problem. He was a Filipino who, at a glance, 'looked' Japanese. Now, I have been repeatedly told by Japanese that they never mistake another Asian for a Japanese like we Westerners are wont to do. But I can also testify that on numerous occasions Japanese proprietors mistook my boss for one of them. They most certainly expected him to be able to speak the language and became agitated when I would communicate on his behalf.

Also, the Japanese do not tend to be particularly respectful of Koreans, although there is a large population who have lived there for generations. My Japanese friends were most insistent that the difference in appearance was obvious to anyone and refused to believe that on two occasions I was seated next to a Korean on a Japan Airlines flight. Both gentlemen asked me to request the hostess to speak to them in English as they didn't understand a word of Japanese.

BUSINESS COMMUNICATION

First, apply everything about interpersonal communication to business communication, which is really only an accumulation of individual interactions on a larger scale.

If you are dealing with Japanese in your native tongue, while they are speaking and thinking in one which is foreign to them, you have an obvious advantage. Working in English is a source of power to you and a frustration to them, particularly in contentious situations. Naturally, the reverse is true if you need to conduct business in Japanese.

Translators can serve a useful purpose for both parties. If possible, try to obtain the services of one who has been recommended. It is beneficial if they are a trusted source with no links to the party with which you are negotiating, in order that they can provide post-meeting feedback on some of the meanings behind the phrases used by the other party. It is important that they not only speak both languages well, but can also interpret nuances.

When using a translator, try to keep words and sentences relatively simple. Review any industry-specific technical phrases with them beforehand to ensure there is understanding. They may be reluctant during the meeting to inform you that they do not understand a certain term; which would prove an embarrassment to them in front of both parties. Speak slowly and do not say more than a couple of sentences without a sufficient pause, in order that the person may translate accurately.

Accurate translation is easier said than done. IBM's basic belief is simply stated as 'respect for the individual'. Each of the 350 000 employees throughout the world would be able to articulate that belief, which is fundamental to the human resource principles and practices of the company. However, one acquaintance told me that when it was translated into Japanese, the statement literally meant 'to be selfish', which is certainly not as highly regarded a sentiment to instil amongst employees!

Many books state that Japanese businessmen have translators on hand even though they, themselves, speak perfect English. It is seen as a mere ploy to gain more thinking time and is considered a devious tactic by Westerners. But, if you think about it, it really makes a lot of sense and there is nothing wrong with giving somewhat more consideration and allowing more time to digest information.

A prompt reply from you or a Japanese person is not necessarily expected whereas in the West, any delay may be seen as slow thinking or a lack of confidence.

In business dealings, especially with the Japanese, silence is truly golden. It is a most useful communication tool and highly recommended when you wish to avoid saying something potentially offensive if you disagree with someone's opinion, don't wish to compromise, or believe they are being unreasonable.

The Japanese are masters at the art of silence in negotiation. You may put forth a point of view which you believe to be a logical, conclusive statement and expect a reply; only to be greeted by absolute silence from your audience. I initially found this hard to cope with but gradually learned to literally bite my tongue (which is a similar texture to raw fish) and dig my nails into the chair in an attempt to restrain myself for what seemed like hours in a crowded, but hushed, room while awaiting a response. It seemed like an eternity but was probably a matter of a few minutes—or even seconds.

Within an organisation, there are many meetings but very little brainstorming as we know it in Western business. There is a reluctance to be even mildly critical of higher management and a hesitation to approach them with ideas or complaints. It is easy to gain consensus if a superior is in the room as people seldom differ with his (and it usually is a male) stated opinion. That is why the informal process of lobbying beforehand is the key to successful meetings. In one to one situations, there is the opportunity for more open discussion, in that no one stands to lose face in front of others.

Should there be any points of disagreement, the Japanese usually prefer to express differences in a very vague sense because frankness can be considered offensive. Whereas contention is often seen as healthy in Western negotiations, Japanese disagreement in public could mean the end to a business relationship or friendship. No wonder there is often confusion with variations in cross-cultural business conduct.

Akio Morita, Chairman of Sony, tells his fellow Japanese that as long as Westerners argue with you, it is okay but when they refuse to talk, the danger point has arrived. He says: 'If Westerners and Japanese are to understand each other, Japanese will need to become as frank as the Americans in putting forth their point of view and Westerners will need to be more tolerant and diplomatic.'

My diplomacy was put to a rigorous test during my first week in the Tokyo office. One of my senior male staff insisted on calling me a 'beautiful' person whenever I asked for his opinion. I had images of being the first female manager in the history of Japan (and probably

4 5

IBM) accused of sexual harassment. I wasn't sure how to handle this and as I was pondering it, discovered that his English was poor and he really meant a 'good' person, which was somewhat of a relief. I had to insist that another staff member stop calling me 'Sir' but there is an important lesson in these two extremes. In fact, much to my surprise, both individuals turned out to be among the very best employees I had the honour to work with.

It is an easy trap to rely on individuals within the organisation who are the most fluent in English and you feel more 'comfortable' with. It is important that you keep their linguistic skills in context and do not necessarily equate that with good business judgement. Do not assume that a competent English speaker is necessarily smarter than colleagues who struggle with the language. Remember that in the West, students who do well at languages are seldom the same ones who excel in sciences. Make the effort to actively listen to those who may not communicate as clearly but have more substance to their message and are not merely what some Japanese refer to as 'English-speaking incompetents' who possess few other practical skills.

Learn to be a better listener. This will gain you a great deal of respect. Loud, aggressive and uncompromising behaviour doesn't win friends or influence people in Japan.

In communications, the Japanese epitomise the concept of promising very little but delivering a lot—*if* the circumstances prove favourable. On the other hand, most Westerners tend to vocalise up-front promises in an attempt to create a good impression; expectations, which for reasons beyond their control, may not always be met.

Eye contact with a superior used to be considered rude and a sign of disrespect but that has also changed with the acceptance of more Western modes of presentation. However, there are still some who find direct eye contact very uncomfortable. Unlike the West, where we're told not to trust someone who can't look you in the eye, it is certainly not the case in Japan.

As for formal business communications, this may vary greatly between firms. You may see the traditional staff stand up meeting before the premises open each morning or the sophisticated company video which is distributed by management to communicate their current message. There could be company newsletters, bulletin boards or kick-off meetings to launch new products or a new year.

If your business is involved in mass communication with customers, you obviously must determine the best means of serving that particular audience. I was amused at one form letter I received which read:

> Dear Mr Catherine . . . When we recently mailed your certificate, we accidentally enclosed a letter in Japanese. We now assume you can not read Japanese, so have enclosed herewith the letter in English. We profoundly apologise for any inconvenience this may have caused.

It goes without saying that it is important to have good translations of all business material, and at least one thoroughly fluent bilingual staff member.

The American Chamber of Commerce in Japan publishes a telephone directory in English, which contains the telephone numbers of such services as airlines, bookstores, churches, delivery companies, hospitals, hotels, physicians, pharmacies, sports, radio stations, consulates, rates of charges for overseas calls etc. This is a very useful communication tool but just because that particular business is listed in that directory, do not assume that you will automatically get an English-speaking person on the other end of the phone.

One last word of advice on communication. It is very simply the Golden Rule. Treat other people as you would like to be treated . . . in any country. I was horrified when a Malaysian colleague informed me that an American colleague insisted on saying '*Ohayo gozaimasu*' (good morning in Japanese) to the office staff in Kuala Lumpur; and justified his total insensitivity by saying: 'What's wrong? I'm talking Asian to them!'. I'm sure that's not how he would have liked to be treated by a visitor to his country!

One of the loveliest expressions came from a tour guide who was showing us through an ancient temple. He explained that the stream leading to the temple contained purified water and confidently informed us: 'If you drink this water, you will live until . . . you die!'

There would be little legal liability in a statement such as that.

So, 'If you follow this advice on communication, you will be okay until . . . you make a mistake.'

Refer also to: Business cards, Bowing, Decisions, Discretion . . . and loss of face, Meetings, Names, Patience, X-pats, Yes

D

DEATH

Death of a loved one is traumatic under any circumstances but even more stressful when not in familiar surroundings. It is hoped you never need to refer to this section of the book so all details of sending corpses to a home country etc. are not covered, as your consulate would help in such a circumstance. It is only essential to know the following:

- Do not move the body.
- Contact the police.
- Contact the doctor.
- Contact your clergy.
- Contact your embassy.

Refer also to: Funerals

DECISIONS

How often do you hear Westerners voice frustration with the seemingly endless decision-making process in Japan? That anxiety stems from the totally different approach which the two cultures have to negotiation.

The Japanese inevitably take a very long time to arrive at a firm decision. That's the bad news. The good news is that once consensus is finally reached (and it is admittedly a long, frustrating process), the implementation of the proposal proceeds without delay. It's full steam ahead to translate plans into actions because prior approvals have been gained at all levels and in different sectors of the or-ganisation to ensure the situation is fully com-prehended. Because likely problems and contingencies are considered well in advance, it is unlikely the decision will later be altered as a result of unforeseen difficulties.

This is the direct opposite to the Western approach where we are anxious to agree in principle as soon as possible; and prior to implementation, may discover all sorts of unexpected reasons for delays, changes etc. How often do we use phrases such as 'Let's look at the big picture', 'All we really need is a ball park figure' or 'Let's agree to the concept and have the staffies work out the details later'?

So, one can fully appreciate why the Japanese must become equally frustrated with Western decision-making, which always seem to include unexpected changes long after they believe final agreement has been reached.

Naturally, there are a lot of meetings involved in any decision-making process and the section on meetings will cover some protocols in more detail. On all these occasions, there is a great deal of emphasis on personal relationships and trust. A significant amount of time should initially be spent building rapport through discussions of family, hobbies etc.

Wa is the Japanese equivalent of harmony and should be maintained at all times. One should never appear confrontational in discussions, regardless of personal frustration. Any disagreements should be voiced quietly and calmly; and always in private. Never force someone to take a decision in public. This advice applies not only to potential trading partners but also to your own staff.

If you feel a need to criticise personnel, do so in a manner which will allow them to save face. Try to encourage them to personally reflect on how their behaviour could be altered for a better result; rather than be abusive which may only serve to make them angry or defensive, and thus not at all receptive to improvement.

In negotiations, don't be surprised if an issue which you thought was already settled comes up again. The obvious temptation is to argue openly and become annoyed that the matter has resurfaced. Refrain from doing so. Simply state surprise that it has been raised and indicate that you will again need to consult with your colleagues. This shows you are giving their point of view due consideration. If you outwardly refute a particular point, it could be implied you were not giving it the attention warranted and slighting the person who offered that view.

Akio Morita, Chairman of Sony, says, 'I think Americans must learn to compromise and listen more' (Morita, A. *Made in Japan*, Collins). He adds, 'In Japan, the most successful leader in business is not the man who goes around giving detailed instructions to his subordinates. It is the man who gives his subordinates only general guidelines and instils confidence in them and helps them to do good work' (Morita, A. *Made in Japan*, Collins).

This helps explain why the key decision-maker may not be involved in all the preliminary negotiation.

During or near the end of negotiations, you may be asked for an inordinate amount of detailed data, which may not seem pertinent to the overall decision. One underlying reason for this degree of detail would be to document all the rationale behind the decision on a formal file note. This would be useful if it was necessary to later justify the decision and allow the decision-makers (and there usually are more than one!) to save face should the venture not work out as expected.

A formal ceremony sometimes plays a part in finalising an agreement once a decision is eventually reached. Seek advice from Japanese counterparts if this is the expectation in regard to the particular deal you have struck. If deemed appropriate, this meeting should be attended by the highest ranking manager of each organisation, as well as all who participated in the actual negotiations. It is also wise to determine the expectations of the extravagance of the ceremony as these events may be accompanied by elaborate banquets, photographs, speeches, gifts etc. However, this is becoming less the norm and seldom expected if the actual signing occurs on your territory.

Nashikuzushi is a Japanese term which dictates you should not suddenly announce any change in company policy. If you believe changes are required, it is more subtle to simply pretend the original policy is still intact but subject to minor changes. These 'minor changes' may in fact be so many that the original policy eventually ceases to exist and is virtually replaced by the approach you advocated all along.

'Death by a thousand cuts' is the very descriptive samurai warrior translation used to explain this approach. It means that you make a few painless little cuts, until eventually the body loses so much blood from these thousands of apparently harmless scratches that the accumulative effect results in death.

Decisions are ultimately made with due consideration to a number of critical factors. However, in Japan, a business relationship built on friendship and trust generally proves more valuable than one that is simply price-sensitive.

Refer also to: Discretion . . . and loss of face, Meetings, Obligation, Patience, Teamwork, Tradition, Unions, Yes

DISCRETION . . . AND LOSS OF FACE

It is important never to cause anyone to 'lose face' when dealing with Japanese. This traditionally meant that one should always show outward respect to an individual, especially a superior, even if such respect was not warranted. Many Japanese still adhere to this reverence to more senior staff but it is no longer a universal practice to agree automatically with someone simply because of their position in the organisation. However, it is still essential that you never criticise anyone in public nor raise your voice in discussions. By the way, this isn't bad advice to follow when doing business in any country.

Be careful not to criticise other people or other people's ideas. In the West, we usually (but not always!) accept constructive criticism of our ideas. We do not take it personally if criticism is offered in a non-emotive, objective way with suggestions for improvement. Most managers are comfortable with some form of brain-storming to improve an original concept and seldom expect their first proposal to be adopted in entirety without alterations.

In Japan, there is a greater likelihood that any criticism of a business plan or idea could be taken as a personal criticism of the individual who made the submission. Therefore, if there is a problem with a proposal, it is a challenge to determine how to make modifications without implying criticism. I wish I could suggest some magic formula to do so. It is not that simple, but try to refrain from dismissing an idea outright. You may wish to nod and say that is an interesting suggestion and then ask for their opinion of your comments.

For example, rather than say ' I don't think that will work because . . . ' say: 'That is a very interesting idea which I think we should fully investigate. I also have an idea which I would welcome your views on so we can come up with the most desirable overall solution which is best for everyone'.

The Japanese comfortably differentiate between reality and a socially acceptable facade. *Tatemae* is the acceptable facade. *Honne* is the reality or hidden truth. Embracing the *honne* philosophy allows governments, organisations and individuals to conscientiously avoid revealing the precise, entire truth, without repercussion. In other words, they can still tell the 'truth' without telling the 'truth, the whole truth and nothing but the truth'.

For example, you may hear the legend of the establishment of Toyota Motor Company whereby the founder sold his only asset, a weaving loom, to raise capital for Japan's first car factory. This is the *tatemae*, the acceptable facade. What you are unlikely to hear is the other side of the story whereby the Japanese government actually provided half of the capital to the company and gave it tax-free concessions for five years. These actions, in essence, forced General Motors and Ford out of the Japanese market. That is the *honne*, the reality of the hidden truth. That is not to detract, for a moment, from the tremendous success of Toyota, but simply to illustrate a common reluctance to openly discuss the less favourable aspect of any situation.

The concept of *honne* also applies to unisex toilets. Oftentimes, I would blush when emerging from a cubicle to meet a man at a urinal. But, as far as the Japanese are concerned, there is no cause for embarrassment when encountering a member of the opposite sex in such a situation. The person is simply seen as invisible. They are not noticed because they are not really there, so there is no need for embarrassment?!?

Many Western friends would voice their annoyance that Japanese always pretended to be polite and friendly in a working environment; but behind your back, you were secretly resented as a Westerner. I honestly can't comment whether that is true or not. Quite frankly, I didn't care. I would much prefer to have people outwardly helpful and not know what they said behind my back than have them be uncooperative and abrasive to my face. Maybe my staff really did think I was nothing more than a dumb *gaijin* but they certainly never gave me that impression.

Titles are very important in Japan. Within any organisation, the title on one's business card should be indicative of status within the hierarchy. It is common that titles are designed to at least create an illusion of advancement within a company. Fortunately, the title which appeared on my business card was of sufficient stature to compensate for the obvious fact that I was a female.

Some companies may still expect employees to address a manager by their title rather than their name. For example, one would greet the chief executive officer as 'President-*san*' (Mr President) rather than 'Matsumoto-*san*' (Mr Matsumoto).

Concern about loss of face was one key reason why automatic teller machines were slow to be fully utilised in

Japan. When they were first installed, they were only operative during banking hours so they could be readily repaired if any problem arose. This resulted from the stated fear that if one such machine ran out of cash, a newspaper could report it and that particular bank would lose face. Losing face is so serious that the government actually dictated banks only opened automatic teller machines when they could be fully staffed, thus diminishing some of the obvious productivity gains.

I recall two incidents where I unintentionally caused other individuals to lose face. The first instance was when a very thin man slipped down a gap on the subway platform. I was astounded that no one nearby rushed to help him before an oncoming train was likely to arrive. I ran over and invoked the assistance of two rather reluctant bystanders as we pulled him up. I was amazed that he didn't offer a word of thanks. I learned later that this was due to two factors. He not only experienced embarrassment and loss of face; but the other two Japanese guys had apparently ignored him because they didn't want to force a feeling of indebtedness. I had some difficulty comprehending this totally different reaction to what I would have had if someone had rescued me from danger. I was equally bemused when, some weeks later, I fell asleep during my language lesson. My teacher dismissed my apologies and remorse saying, 'No, it is I who should apologise for being such a boring teacher'. It all relates to loss of face. I felt so embarrassed for making her lose face, that I never again dozed.

Refer also to: Bowing, Business cards, Communication . . . and useful phrases, Names, Obligation, Patience, Resignation and retrenchment, Seniority, Tradition, Yes

E

EARTHQUAKES

Unlike a typhoon, an earthquake strikes without warning. Therefore preparation for earthquakes must be considered years in advance. Everyone should be completely familiar and thoroughly drilled with the required actions to take should a 'big one' occur.

The government has an elaborate emergency plan. Designated refuge areas and maps are displayed on street corners to show people where to go. Unfortunately for the Westerner, these are only written in Japanese. So, what precautions should one take?

PRE-EARTHQUAKE PREPARATION

The Minato Ku (a suburb of Tokyo) has an English-language audio tape of the actions to take before, during and after an earthquake. A copy can be obtained by taking a blank cassette into that office.

There are also a few publications published by the Tokyo Fire Department which have been translated into English. A booklet *Protecting Yourself in an Earthquake* is available from the American Chamber of Commerce office in Tokyo. The American Red Cross in California also publishes a comprehensive booklet.

It would be worthwhile to take time to familiarise yourself with such information. It would also be wise to have a documented emergency plan for your workplace and the occasional earthquake drill; not unlike regular fire drills which Westerners accept as normal procedure.

IBM went to great lengths to provide all employees with basic provisions which could be useful in the event of an earthquake. It was definitely over the top to have huge, red letters 'Earthquake Survival Kit' prominently displayed on the outside of this canvas bag. I personally don't believe it is a company responsibility to prepare such a kit but it is obviously worthwhile to inform foreign employees of precautions which can be taken to reduce danger to themselves and families.

The following checklist is one which should be considered by any individual living in Tokyo and the necessary goods stored together in an easily accessible place in case of emergency:

- Printed information on what to expect and what to do
- Transistor radio and batteries
- Drinking water and purification tablets
- Warm clothing and sturdy shoes
- Blanket
- First aid kit
- Personal hygiene supplies
- Dehydrated, non-perishable or canned food
- Can opener
- Paper plates and plastic utensils
- Soap
- Watch

- Money
- Essential medication
- Large plastic garbage bags
- Toilet paper
- Waterproof matches
- Swiss army knife
- Pen and paper
- Don't forget provisions for your pets
- Always have a fire extinguisher on hand and know how to use it.

It is actually the fires after the earthquake which usually cause more damage, so ensure that you know how to extinguish all pilot lights, flames etc.

DURING THE EARTHQUAKE

* Don't panic. This is easier said than done, especially during your first one! I couldn't believe how calm my boss, a five-year veteran of Japan, was when I experienced my first tremor. To this day, I can vividly remember sitting in his office, watching the outside street lamps waver like toothpicks and feeling the multistorey building shake. He carried on with the meeting in progress as if nothing had happened. As I was about to bite my fingernails beyond recognition he casually commented 'Don't worry, it's just a little one'. It did, in fact, register 6.9 on the Richter scale, which is a sufficiently high reading to cause massive devastation in areas with poor construction but Tokyo buildings have been specifically constructed to withstand much greater strain.

* I surprised myself many months later, when I was also calm and capable of reassuring my own staff. It is important for managers in an organisation to keep their cool and exhibit leadership, particularly in such stressful times.

* If you are inside when an earthquake strikes, stay inside. Take cover in a doorway or under a desk or table. This does not look at all dignified but is an appropriate action to take—not because a flimsy table will necessarily protect you if the floor above collapses, but it *will* protect you in the much more likely event of shattering glass.

* Stay away from windows, mirrors or china cabinets. The obvious temptation is to look out the windows to see what is happening. This is the worst thing to do as shattered glass is quite common.

* Don't be surprised if the fire alarm and sprinkler systems come on in the building.

* Douse all open flames and don't use candles or matches.

* If you're outside, try to move away from utility wires and tall buildings. If possible (and even at the best of times, it seems impossible in Tokyo) try to find an open space away from buildings. Don't run near buildings as the greatest danger is from falling debris.

* If you are in a car, you are less likely to feel an earthquake. But, if you do feel a tremor, stop the vehicle as soon as it is safe to do so and remain in the car.

* If you are in a subway, don't panic if the train stops and the lights go out. This can be quite disconcerting but people kept reassuring me that the underground was one of the safest places to be during an earthquake as the construction had been especially reinforced. I was never convinced but

there was little I could do, so remaining calm seemed the best option.

AFTER THE EARTHQUAKE

• If you smell gas, shut off the main valve, leave the building and report the leak to the authorities.

• If the water supply is damaged, shut it off at the mains.

• If there is even a minor electrical problem, shut off the fuse box.

• Stay off the telephone except to report an emergency.

• Listen to the English radio station for possible instructions.

• Open cupboard doors carefully as things may fall out.

• If you live along the coast, proceed to the highest ground as it is possible a tidal wave could hit soon after the earthquake.

All of these above precautions became firmly planted in my mind as a result of living in Japan. When an earthquake hit NSW, Australia, in 1989, I was horrified when people ran from high rise buildings and stood in the street looking skyward, when debris could have been falling. But I would have done exactly the same if I hadn't been exposed to the threat of such a natural disaster.

Refer also to: Safety and security, Typhoons

EDUCATION AND TRAINING

There are a number of excellent international schools in Tokyo and children of expatriates should not be at all disadvantaged in their schooling by the move. In fact, they stand to gain in a much broader educational sense by the mere virtue of experiencing another culture. As in any environment, some students find it more difficult than others to adjust to any change and a few 'expat brats' are the result. However, most children will adapt more readily than their parents; especially if their parents consistently demonstrate a positive attitude towards the changes they themselves experience.

As excellent as the education is, the foreign-speaking schools are all independent and therefore without tax support, so the fees are very high.

The international schools are predominantly based in the main cities and lists with up-to-date details and facilities would be available from your consulate or the United States Consulate in Tokyo.

The academic year is from September until mid June and the school day is normally 8.15 a.m. to 3.15 p.m., five days a week.

Although entrance requirements vary, a transcript and health report from the child's previous school is often required. There are few provisions for children with special needs.

TRAINING IN THE WORKPLACE

The Japanese have an average intelligence quotient (IQ) of 111, which is the highest recorded for a national population, according to a 1982 study. Whereas Americans and Europeans have 2 per cent of their population with IQs over 130, the Japanese have 10 per cent at this level (Lynn, R. 'IQ in Japan and US Shows a Growing Disparity', *Nature*, May 20, 1982 p. 222).

Can that explain why Japan consistently outperformed the West on the economic front in the 1980s? I think not. The answer more likely lies in their commitment to continuing education and training.

In 1950, about 1 per cent of new entrants into the labour force had attended institutes of higher learning. In 1980, that figure had climbed to an outstanding 40 per cent. In spite of this huge increase in the quantity of graduates, there are still extensive comments in the media from organisations who are unhappy with the quality of graduates their universities are producing. That is but one reason for in-depth company training programs.

The amount and variety of education provided for employees exceeds that found in any other nation. Much of the education is aimed at creating and reinforcing attitudes, as well as skills training.

Just as in Western countries, the quality and quantity of training varies between different organisations.

Although times are changing, it is safe to say that in most instances, training is much more extensive for male workers than females since it is considered a better investment, based on the assumption of a longer-term contribution to the work force over time.

Those Japanese companies which have a lifetime employment policy are obviously conscious of the need for extensive employee development. Within the first week of joining such an organisation, newcomers would participate in a comprehensive orientation program. The content and duration of the sessions would vary enormously but would aim to familiarise recruits with not only the operational aspects, but the philosophy and traditions of the firm. Programs could last days, weeks or even months to ensure the new employee fully comprehends the nature of the business as well as the written and unwritten codes of conduct.

After that, it is common to have annual or semi-annual updates, supposedly to further educate the employees about the current state of the business and personnel practices in the company. These are compulsory and usually take the form of a two to three day retreat at an *onsen* (country spa resort). A bus is chartered and the most senior manager may engage in a role-reversal exercise by handing out bags of nibblies to each member as the trip commences, a trip which aims to foster better teamwork. At these functions, the group is encouraged to spend virtually every waking moment together in some form of organised activity. It is not uncommon for them to also bathe and sleep together on the floor of a communal room—one for males and one for females. Spouses are seldom invited.

Alcohol consumption is considered normal on these excursions to help break down barriers and allow workers to be more open in their communications. All actions under the influence of alcohol are meant to be immediately forgotten upon return to the office.

There is also specialised training in technical and job-specific courses. Some is done by company training departments and some contracted externally. Employees who have been earmarked as potential management may be sent overseas to attend a training program. As well as gaining skills, this may be seen as a reward for effort and indicative that the company values that employee. With increased globalisation, more companies are sending younger managers overseas for longer term assignments. It is also becoming commonplace for companies trading internationally to hold annual offshore seminars. This allows middle and senior managers of those overseas divisions to meet with head office staff for a formal update on the business.

However, the most predominant means by which Japanese companies develop employee skills is by providing a good deal of ongoing, cross-functional training and job rotation. This not only increases the competencies of staff but is invaluable in breaking down traditional interdepartmental barriers, such as the classic clashes between marketing and production. Employees gain increased understanding of the overall business operation which should ultimately provide increased productivity. In addition, the high fliers are exposed to all aspects of the company so that a greater number should have the potential to move into general management. This is possible because the organisational structure is somewhat less vertical than the traditional pyramid-shaped hierarchy adhered to by most Western management.

A Japanese company may provide a study grant for a promising executive to study overseas; because it is safe to say that the Japanese are just as fascinated by Western management style as we are by theirs . . . if not more so. The difference is that more of their young people have been able to gain ready admission to American, British and Australian universities by virtue of their language skills and high academic grades in accord with entry specifications. Until recently, few Westerners have had the ability or opportunity to study at Japanese tertiary institutes so the mystery of Japanese management techniques remains thus.

We have an interesting perspective in this regard. What we consider to be successful Japanese methodologies may, in fact, have actually been copied from the West. The most obvious example is the approach to quality for which the Japanese have become world renowned. The basis for quality circles was, in fact, devised by an American by the name of Dr W. E. Deming. His theories were originally rejected in the West and accepted in Japan. The rest is history but some Westerners remain mystified by the Japanese 'secret' in this regard.

Nowadays, it is common for firms to fund out-of-office English classes for employees wishing to invest their own time developing this language skill. Continued funding is provisional upon successful completion of exams as study progresses. Assistance in full or partial financing of part-time, job-related study is also becoming more common.

Because of the principle of lifelong employment, training costs are amortised over a long career so the Japanese are not hesitant to invest substantial amounts in training because of anticipated payback. Development of employees is very much regarded as an investment; rather than a cost.

Refer also to: Hygiene factors, Internationalism, Lifelong employment, Quality, Recruiting

ENTERTAINMENT

Not unlike the West, there are obligatory business entertainment expectations—to entertain customers, visitors from head office, suppliers etc.

However, the distinction between leisure and work in Japan is somewhat more blurred. Workers frequently socialise out of hours, with the expressed purpose of cementing business relationships. This may simply be a few cold drinks with colleagues; or the entire team going out to dinner, followed by games of *mahjong* or *pachinko* (a form of one-armed bandit).

According to the Institute of Statistical Mathematics in their 1986 'Study of the National Japanese Character', games, gambling and dining out are classified as business entertainment. It accounts for 53 per cent of Japanese leisure expenditure.

Spouses are seldom included but like everything else in Japan, this is also changing and depends on the situation.

Many of my Western male colleagues were naturally fascinated with the notion of geisha bars. Admittedly, I was a foreign female in a male-dominated Japanese business environment, but I saw little evidence that these were the definitive norm of entertainment. There can be no denying that geisha bars are indeed quite popular and lucrative businesses in themselves. But the Western myth (no doubt perpetated by wishful-thinking males!) portrays all Japanese businessmen as frequenting these establishments on a daily basis before stumbling home to their wives. This does, in fact, occur and must account in some part for the number of inebriated salary men (office workers) seen staggering on the last midnight train. However, to present a more balanced view, it must be remembered that there are literally millions more who have been home with their families for many hours.

I personally visited geisha bars on only a few occasions but then again, I would seldom be seen in a pub in Australia, so I'm not sure if any generalisations can be drawn; although the proportion of men to women was certainly more pronounced in Japan. I was accompanied by male colleagues on each visit and they were obviously 'regulars' at the establishment as they had their own, personally labelled bottle of high-quality Scotch whisky which was produced upon our arrival. However, these particular 'regulars' claimed they hadn't visited the bar for some months and the attending geisha likewise made comments to the effect that she hadn't seen them for some time.

It led me to the conclusion that drunkenness after work is not a prerequisite for successful business dealings in Japan. In fact, Akio Morita, the Chairman of Sony, does not drink at all. So, it seems that this 'need' to get drunk to be successful in Japanese business dealings may be a myth perpetuated by those who 'want' to indulge; just as some Australian men will claim the 'need' for the boys to get together for a beer after work.

Having said all this, there is little doubt that socialising over a drink can be very pleasant and assist in creating more relaxed business communications. *Kampai* means 'cheers' in Japanese. It is a useful icebreaker to have in your limited vocabulary.

Stories are told of Japanese businessmen who entertain in shifts and pace themselves while the sole Westerner gets outrageously drunk and is, subsequently, in a weakened bargaining position the following morning. This is probably true but I've only personally spoken to one businessman who has had such an experience. And even he, after his head recovered, was willing to admit that he could have showed somewhat more restraint by emptying his glass more slowly.

If hosting a group of local businesspeople in Tokyo, don't even attempt to pinpoint the 'right' sort of Japanese restaurant. Japanese executives relish dining at fine continental establishments. Top restaurants at large hotels are the safest bet for quality food and service to impress Japanese counterparts. They won't be cheap but you have more control over the situation because the staff usually speak English. Bookings should be made in advance for formal entertaining.

For more casual dining, Japanese colleagues provide the best guide to local restaurants, which are inevitably tucked away in some back alley where a visitor would never venture. Some of the most sumptuous meals were eaten in places that I reluctantly entered with colleagues—be open minded and you will usually be pleasantly surprised.

When entertaining or being entertained, you should not pour your own drink. Never let the glass of an acquaintance remain empty and always lift your glass or sake cup when someone pours for you.

Tipping is not required but there will usually be a service charge added to the bill.

As for payment of the bill, I must confess that I never determined an exact standard of conduct for doing so. Obviously, if you invited a client, you would pick up the tab and vice versa. But, in situations when work mates would gather, the bill was sometimes split, people took turns hosting the evening or the boss might pay.

In one establishment, each individual paid by the hour for an unlimited amount of food and beer which they could consume in that time period.

Another less common form of entertainment would be for colleagues to visit a live sex show on their way home from the office. This is definitely not the norm but it's probably safe to say that most males would have attended at some stage and be urged on by their buddies to actually become a participant in the show; where attendees can vie for the opportunity to star on stage.

At the opposite extreme, some workers may gather after hours at an 'oxygen bar' in a department store. Here, you can partake of three minutes of pure oxygen for 100 yen (1$A) or spend 750 yen for a two-minute take-away can. Oxygen flavours come in coffee, mushroom, mint and lemon! Over 15 000 take-away cans are sold per month. I suspect it's just a fad and not likely to ever catch on as a substitute for alcohol.

It's also unlikely that 'aqua bars' will ever replace the more traditional watering hole. However, in one of the latest trends, patrons actually line up at long wooden counters, as a bartender pours shots from a wide range of domestic and imported brands of vogue mineral water.

Bars in Japan are small and crowded so major companies are understandably emphatic that employees should be cautious about what they discuss in environments where tongues are oiled by alcohol and conversation could be easily overheard by a competitor. Intellectual property is too valuable to be lost in this manner. Sony actually founded a non-profit bar on its own premises to help prevent information leaks. This still allows for out of hours camaraderie and has the added bonus of reducing the expense claims of managers entertaining subordinates.

The opening of new offices is a cause for great celebration. Banks are noted for the most elaborate functions, but almost any office worth its salt will invite customers to a lavish event to mark the occasion. I once attended the relocation of a furniture rental company and was amazed at the presence of ostentatious flower arrangements, which made me feel I was entering a funeral parlour rather than a party. I later learned that most of the huge bouquets would have been sent by attendees at the party (except for ignorant me!) or suppliers of that company wishing it well for the future. The food was elaborate and every guest received a very chic gift when they left.

Sumo and golf are also popular ways to entertain clients in Japan. Entertaining customers at cultural events gives companies the added advantage of prestige in the community. Major companies may actually subsidise public concerts. The Suntory Concert Hall in Tokyo is a case in point. Many overseas artists are invited but even with corporate sponsorship, tickets can cost as much as US$500 per concert! Some large firms have their own galleries while others sponsor artistic exhibitions in department stores. Like any sponsorship commitment in the West, these are analysed on a cost–benefit to the corporation.

The National Tax Administration Agency keeps tabs on company entertainment. Official statistics were published in a 1987 newspaper report stating that corporations spent a record 3.94 billion yen on entertainment, which was up 2.5 per cent from the previous year.

Most business entertaining is conducted at commercial premises such as restaurants or hotels. This is partially due to the prestige and convenience of doing so, and partially because the Japanese home may be too small or the person embarrassed by its size compared to a Westerner's abode. However, do not believe that you will never receive an invitation to a Japanese home.

I was told that would be the case but within only two weeks of my arrival, a neighbour invited me to dinner with his family. Neither his wife nor children spoke any English but he acted as a translator. I received a number of such invitations.

Etiquette dictates that you should always take the hostess a small gift. This is not unlike our custom of taking a bottle of wine, box of chocolates or flowers to dinner. However, a key difference in Japan is that the token of appreciation must be properly gift wrapped.

When entering a home or traditional restaurant, it is important to remove one's shoes. You will usually find them conveniently turned around when you leave. You would look silly removing your shoes in the Japanese equivalent of a fast-food place. So, if you're not sure . . .

don't be the first to enter the premises.

The most honoured guest at a meal will usually be seated with their back to the *tokonoma*. This is an area where the household's prized possessions are usually displayed. The seats closest to the door are for those lowest in rank and usually occupied by the host. You should not necessarily take the first seat offered to you, particularly if it is the seat of honour.

Similar to Western custom, one would usually be well dressed for a meal. However, in some *ryokan*s (small inns), you may actually get *un*dressed for dinner. The establishment will provide you with a *yukata* (patterned, cotton dressing gown) after a bath. Every other patron in the dining room will wear the same attire. It is very relaxing to eat in this manner but important to check what the norm is; because if you were to dine at a top hotel in your *yukata*, it would be equally embarrassing to you, the management and other guests.

Many Japanese have spent a great deal of time in Western entertainment environments and homes. For others, it is a novelty and they are not sure how to react. So, be prepared for anything as a host unless you know the people are familiar with Western traditions. Let me cite two extremes.

One young man arrived for a dinner party with a huge family sized box of Kentucky Fried Chicken and no less than three bottles of Australian wine as he wanted to appear Westernised and reciprocate my hospitality. I felt obliged to serve the Colonel Sanders along with the gourmet meal I had prepared, so as not to offend him.

At the other extreme, one woman arrived at the door

and much to my amazement had also brought her sister and three children. That evening was a case of 'Guess who's coming to dinner?' as I attempted a loaves and fishes culinary miracle. I only wished I'd invited the Kentucky Fried Chicken man on the same occasion!

When entertaining Japanese, remember that they usually arrive before the prescribed time. This can be a surprise for the host, in the midst of last minute preparations, who is accustomed to Western guests arriving a fashionable fifteen minutes late.

Refer also to: Baseball, Food, Gift giving, Golf, Karaoke, Lunches, Parties, Sport and recreation, Women, Work ethic

ENVIRONMENT

Much international media attention has been focused on Japan's whaling industry as environmentally irresponsible. Few would realise that they took the lead in the 1970s to require domestic garbage be separated into paper, bottles, cans and other for recycling.

Speaking of the environment . . . the Japanese nation has a reverence for Mount Fuji. It is a beautiful, perfectly shaped conical peak which can occasionally be seen through the industrial haze. A large percentage of the population aspire to climb to its 3776 metre summit. This may even be done as a company team-building exercise. The night I made the ascent to see the sunrise, the path up the volcanic slope seemed more crowded than the Ginza. It was bumper-to-bumper people of all ages, with miners' head lamps, walking sticks and cameras.

The price of Coca-Cola escalated with each foot in altitude and one would hardly term the experience as getting away from it all. As I huddled in the cold morning rain and couldn't see more than two feet in front of me, I could only agree with the very apt Japanese proverb describing their revered mountain: 'One is a fool to never climb Fuji. One is a bigger fool to climb twice.'

Refer also to: Sport and recreation

F

FOOD

It is impolite to ask what sort of food you are eating. And sometimes it's preferable not to know! As a semi-vegetarian, I was always able to politely refuse many unappealing dishes on the basis that it was 'against my religion' to eat living creatures. Although this was admittedly not quite true, it saved both my host and me from any embarrassing situation where I otherwise may have been expected to swallow a live fish! You will find that rice is not served until the end of the meal because it is considered the least savoury food and is only brought as a 'filler' once the more interesting food has been consumed. Slurping noodles in restaurants is perfectly acceptable.

Chopsticks are the normal eating utensils which would be provided. I was appalled to learn some Westerners insisted on carrying their own knife and fork when they dined out! Can you imagine the disparaging comments if an Oriental guest arrived at our home or restaurant with chopsticks. On the other hand, I still found it mildly condescending when a Japanese would comment 'You use chopsticks very well'.

I refrained from counteracting with, 'Thanks, you use a spoon very well'.

Most Japanese meals tend to be on the salty side which understandably results in consumption of large quantities of liquid refreshment. Water is usually provided and is completely safe to drink but most diners seem to prefer beer or sake (hot or cold).

No tip is expected in restaurants although in more up-market, Westernised establishments, this is becoming common. However, in the majority of instances, a service charge is added to the bill. Even in small restaurants, the service is excellent and there sometimes seem to be more waiters than customers in the place. You are provided with a hot or cold towel to refresh you before your meal and cleanse you after—a most welcome respite.

Ordering food can sometimes be a problem if you are not fluent in Japanese. This is largely overcome because most restaurants have surprisingly appetising plastic displays of food in their window. You can simply go outside and point to what you would like.

More than one friend has actually mistaken another customer for a staff member and dragged them outside to point at the display of food. On every occasion, the customer concerned has politely ordered for the Westerner—such is the service mentality whether one is, or is not, the official server.

It is simple to have food delivered to your home, especially if you have a home card, not unlike a business card with your name, address and phone number on the front and map of your location on the back. Once you have established a relationship with your local *soba* (noodles) or *sushi* (raw fish) take-away, they will deliver to your door and leave the lovely lacquered dishes to be picked up later. Even easier is pizza and hamburger delivery which cater to the Western palate and provides all menus and phone numbers in English.

The people delivering the food are always extremely polite. I remember being sick with a dreadful cold one day. My haggard appearance obviously startled the young man who was confronted at the door by this *gaijin* in a dressing gown. He immediately recovered and in broken English said, 'Oh, I am so sorry you look like you feel sick today'.

That apparently genuine concern provided more nourishment than the food.

Company cafeterias are often located on the premises. One of my challenges was to come up with a suitable menu to cater to both Western and Japanese tastes. Most firms wouldn't have enough critical mass of Westerners to worry about this problem. Quite frankly, I think we devoted too much time to it; even though I shared others' aversion to *miso* (bean) soup day in and day out. The Japanese were probably equally repulsed by the offerings of mediocre hamburgers which were supposed to appease the Western palate.

My personal opinion is that it seems a no win situation to run a company cafeteria anywhere in the world, as staff seldom seem happy with the quality of cuisine. I suspect that even if we'd hired a five-star Michelin chef, there would still have been complaints. Even though the cafeteria was heavily subsidised, most of our work force would eat externally at least once or twice a week. That would not be the case in companies which were situated in remote locations. However, in the business area of any major city, you would always find a collection of Japanese at their favourite *soba* shop and groups of Westerners feasting on a hamburger at the American club or McDonald's.

I saw newspaper reports of beef being sold on one occasion for 100 000 yen ($1000) per kilogram. It came from an award winning cow which was sold for 26 million yen! Other reports of the annual crab auction quote individual crabs fetching 45 000 yen each— wholesale! But, please rest assured that the average consumer doesn't need to pay anywhere near that.

When I first arrived in Tokyo, an apple cost the equivalent of A\$2 at a time when I could have purchased two dozen for the same price back home. And rockmelons which would normally retail for about 50 cents in Sydney were an astounding A\$90! After the initial shock, I found that prices usually balanced out in conjunction with the higher wages and one learned to shop for fruit and vegetables in season or eliminate certain foodstuffs as a regular part of the diet. I never did like rockmelon that much anyway!

There were certain foods which were definitely in fashion, for which you paid a premium price. These fads didn't always last but I could never explain why one particular ice-cream store always had a queue of at least 15 minutes and charged twice as much as any other comparable product . . . just another little mystery of Japan for which it's not worth worrying about the answer (unless of course you're in the ice-cream business).

Refer also to: Entertainment, Gift giving, Lunches, Parties, Service

FUNERALS

If you have the misfortune to attend a funeral, there are certain protocols which must be observed. The actual ceremony is often an intimate family occasion, followed by a large wake. These are very formal occasions.

If the eldest son of the deceased is an employee in your company, you may be requested to provide staff of his choosing to attend the funeral. These colleagues will assist with various tasks at the wake, such as collecting money from guests.

Even if you don't know the deceased, you will probably be expected to attend the funeral if a member of the immediate family reports directly to you. However, this would depend on whether the family would feel comfortable with a foreigner present at such a solemn event.

In one instance, a senior Japanese male colleague advised me that I should simply send a telegram and flowers. He indicated it would be appropriate if I gave him the cash donation to represent our department at the funeral. He felt it would be inappropriate for me to go because I did not know the employee very well, it was a very traditional ceremony and few members of the family had exposure to Westerners.

On another occasion, a young female staff member told me about the death of her father. I was surprised at this tearful conversation which lasted over an hour because I had been told that Japanese don't express emotion. I was later informed by a Japanese colleague that this young woman had no right to take my time because she was only a temporary member of staff. Therefore, I had no formal obligation to her. I explained that I would have done the same thing if a similar situation had occurred in Australia. I did what I thought was right; not what I was obliged to do by virtue of tradition or living in Japan.

Refer also to: Death, Gift giving, Obligation

G

GIFT GIVING

Presentos are very popular in Japan. These may be in the form of merchandise or cash.

Management is expected to provide cash gifts to employees who get married, give birth or experience a death in the family. The amount of the gift is dependent on the manager's status in the hierarchy. The higher the level in the organisation, the more expensive the donation.

The donation should take the form of crisp, new bills and always be presented in an attractive envelope which can be bought from any stationery shop. It is important to obtain the appropriate one—for example, don't make the mistake of giving a funeral donation in a wedding envelope. Superstition dictates that bank notes should be in denominations of threes, fives or sevens.

Cash gifts are not cheap. Amounts are likely to be in denominations of hundreds of dollars and possibly more if you are a very senior manager and have a long and close relationship with the individual or their family. If in doubt, seek guidance from a trusted Japanese colleague or friend.

Money is the favoured gift at weddings. This makes a lot of sense as the bride and groom aren't inundated with six toasters and a hideous vase from dear old Aunt Mabel. Apart from whether they like the gift or not, they may simply not have space in their small apartments. When you leave a Japanese wedding, *you* will receive a gift of appreciation from the hosts.

Omiagi is what any employee worth their salt brings back for fellow workers after a business trip or vacation. *Omiagi* consist of beautifully wrapped portions of food, usually unique to a given locality. I personally found some of these regional treats almost inedible as judged by my Western palate. However, as a manager it was important to show that I appreciated the gesture and could always honestly admit that at least it was interesting. It was a welcome relief when staff visited the United States and returned with chocolate-covered macadamia nuts . . . which left no hesitation in expressing appreciation!

By Japanese standards, *omiagi* are not expensive and a very much appreciated gesture. As a management tool, they can provide a variation to MBWA (Management by Walking Around). Instead of leaving the box of goodies with a secretary to distribute, the clever manager will personally wander around the office, distributing the food and using the opportunity to casually chat with employees. If ever formalised, one could refer to it as Management by Eating Around.

You may also give a gift if someone has done you a favour. Beautifully-wrapped food is always a welcome present because the average Japanese home does not have a lot of room to acquire non-consumable knick-knacks.

It is important that any gift is properly wrapped and not just presented in a brown paper bag.

Avoid giving any gift such as flowers or fruit in a group of four because the *kanji* character for four is associated with death.

Likewise, people who are sick will be offended if you send them a plant. It implies that they are rooted to their bed. Brightly coloured bouquets are always a safe bet, but remember that hospitals do not supply containers for cut flowers.

A very valued low-cost gift is to take photographs at social or work occasions. Get multiple prints made and simply send copies and a little note to those involved. The Japanese are very keen on such photographs. Not only will that gift be appreciated at the time, but kept for years to come, as a constant reminder of East—West friendship.

I was surprised to receive gifts for no apparent reason from my cleaning lady. Naturally, I reciprocated and learned later that there is a certain degree of indebtedness involved in gift exchanges and it is always considered good form to be the first to give.

There are a few rather unusual occasions on which one would be expected to give a gift in Japan.

If you are involved in a traffic accident, you should always immediately visit the accident victim with a *Gomen nasai* (apology) present. This is usually in the form of flowers, fruit, candy or Scotch whisky. It can often deter the other party from pressing formal charges, if a suitable apology and promise to pay is extended with the peace offering.

A friend tells the bizarre story of a minor burglary from his apartment. The thief was convicted for petty theft but released on good behaviour because it was his first offence. You can well imagine the astonishment of my friend when the offender arrived at his door a few months later with a beautifully-wrapped box of cookies, as an apology for the inconvenience he had caused!

If you are a golfer and get a hole in one, you may not see

it as a stroke of luck. The repercussions are far more expensive than buying drinks for the bar. You would be expected to buy gifts for everyone. I have no personal experience in this matter but found it amazing that you could actually take out an insurance policy to cover the expense associated with a hole in one!

If you are travelling to Japan, your business acquaintances will always appreciate a gift which is unique to your country and not as readily available in Japan. It is very popular to bring prepacked fresh steak, seafood or exotic fruit. I found Australian chocolates in the shape of koalas to be a big hit for mass distribution. Admittedly, they weren't quite as highly prized as duty-free Scotch whisky.

And if you are going to Tokyo to visit an expatriate living there, it is considerate to ask if they would like any special goods brought from home. I especially welcomed visitors who arrived with a local newspaper or magazine and my favourite brand of chocolate.

Many business establishments will give gifts to customers on the anniversary of a store opening or special occasion. They may also send *presentos* or a card on your birthday but these actions are more related to marketing than required norms.

The younger Japanese are increasingly exchanging gifts for birthdays, Valentine's Day and Christmas (even though it is largely a non-Christian country).

Refer also to: Entertainment, Holidays and festivals, Obligation, Parties

GOLF

Like baseball, golf deserves special mention because the organisational pervasiveness goes well beyond simple individual enjoyment.

Golf club memberships for executives are not simply a prime perk but are actively traded on the stock exchange. Even mediocre clubs cost in excess of one million US dollars. They are, therefore, viewed as an investment and listed as a capital asset on company books.

Executives frequently entertain clients on the fairways. There is ample time to discuss business as there is usually a two-hour break for lunch after nine holes, as well as a communal bath to relax after the game.

It is considered a good investment to speculate on a yet-undeveloped course and purchase membership a few years before the course is even built. The value usually increases upon completion and varies with the proximity to Tokyo and facilities offered. I had the opportunity to purchase one such membership for only US$600 000. It was purely academic as I didn't have that sort of cash readily available, but I later learned that I would have doubled my money on that particular property in less than three years.

There is an increasing number of Japanese women who are taking up golf but some of the clubs are either very backward, or extremely progressive, in regard to equal opportunity . . . they don't have women's tees!

Many of the young female (and male) golfers in Japan seldom play on an actual course. They buy the appropriate clothing and equipment and book a tee time at a multi-tiered driving range in downtown Tokyo. I've sometimes waited two hours and paid US$20 for the privilege of hitting a bucket of balls. But these facilities are very popular. They have their own restaurants, pro shops and video facilities to watch golf lessons or replays of recent tournaments.

Refer also to: Allowances and benefits, Gift giving, Sport and recreation

GROOMING

Japanese are extremely well dressed and place great emphasis on grooming. Even on Saturday or Sunday afternoon strolls down the Ginza or in parks, personal presentation is considered critical. Where else in the world would you see men in suits and women in high heels wandering around a public garden? You may think this has no relation to work but you certainly wouldn't want your employees, colleagues or clients to bump into you and your family looking grubby, whereas, in Australia, it would be quite acceptable for even the managing director of a major firm to be seen in neat shorts and sneakers in a casual weekend environment. If in doubt what to wear to a function, it is better to slightly overdress.

Refer also to: Hygiene factors

H

HOLIDAYS AND FESTIVALS

Most Japanese workers are entitled to 15 days paid vacation from their company as well as the 12 official public holidays.

When referring to holidays in Japan, I make no mention of 'sickies'. Japan has absentee rates lower than any other developed country. I have read articles which claim the average salaried worker takes only half their annual holiday entitlements. The stated reason is that it would put an extra burden on colleagues and would not be viewed favourably. This is undoubtedly true in some organisations but certainly far from the norm.

NATIONAL HOLIDAYS

The following is a list of proclaimed national holidays. If a public holiday falls on a Sunday, the following Monday is generally taken as the day off.

If you are planning any travel within Japan or overseas during any of these times, it is imperative to make bookings well in advance, especially for New Year's and Golden Week.

1 January	*New Year's Day*
2 and 3 January	*Bank Holidays*
15 January	*Coming of Age Day*
11 February	*National Foundation Day*

21 March	*Equinox Day*
29 April	*Greenery Day*
1 May	*May Day (semi holiday)*
3 May	*Constitution Memorial Day*
5 May	*Children's Day*
15 September	*Respect for the Aged Day*
24 September	*Autumn Equinox*
10 October	*Physical Culture/Health Day*
3 November	*Culture Day*
23 November	*Labour Thanksgiving Day*
23 December	*Emperor's Birthday*

Let's now look at the yearly calendar in more detail. There are literally thousands of festivals with religious or historical significance spread in neighbourhoods throughout the country. Never a week would pass that you couldn't find a festival celebrating something—kites, dolls, fireflies, dragons, irises, tea, lanterns etc. However, this segment will deal with a few major ones and instances where there may be some social obligation on behalf of the employer.

1 JANUARY—NEW YEAR'S DAY

The New Year's holiday is one of two occasions during the year when the whole country slows down in an economic sense.

The first day in January marks the beginning of a new animal year. This is based on a cycle of twelve years with twelve different animals. Each animal is symbolic of certain character traits, similar to Zodiac signs. For example, the years 1938, 1950, 1962 and 1984 are all Years of the Tiger.

If you were born in those years, you supposedly have certain characteristics of the tiger. The cycle is as follows:

1994 Dog	2000 Dragon
1995 Boar	2001 Snake
1996 Rat	2002 Horse
1997 Bull	2003 Sheep
1998 Tiger	2004 Monkey
1999 Rabbit	2005 Cock

Individuals and businesses, alike, visibly welcome the arrival of a New Year. Homes and office buildings are decorated with pine boughs, bamboo stalks and plum branches. These are symbols of longevity, constancy and purity. An elaborately twisted rope binds the plum, pine and bamboo together to prevent evil spirits from entering the front door. No respectful business would be without such adornment in the first week of the new year.

Millions of greeting cards are mailed and many businesses (except retail) close down for about a week. Houses are thoroughly cleaned on New Year's Eve and all debts repaid.

The *Tokyo Times* reported:

As many as 79.37 million people visited shrines and temples at midnight on New Year's Eve or during the following day, across the nation to pray for good fortune. This was a four per cent increase on the previous year.

It remains a mystery to me how such a figure could be accurately assessed with so many small temples located in isolated areas. However, every shrine is certainly bustling with crowds and there is a hopeful spirit in the air. This is not unlike Christmas in the West, as people pray for a bright future for their families and companies.

Thirty members of the IBM club in Sendai City brave a cold, winter's January night to pray for the company's success in the coming year. The local festival is known as *Hadaka Odori*. Traditional dress consists of white cotton cloth, straw festoons around the waist, straw sandals, a white cotton headband and a triangular paper gag in the mouth. Worshippers walk an hour from their office, through falling snow, in a long parade to a shrine. Here, they pray for good fortune for the company as they throw New Year's decorations onto the bonfire. Can't you just imagine union workers in Australia or the United Kingdom doing likewise on a voluntary basis, without any demands of time-and-a-half or hardship pay!

On 2 January, the Emperor and his family appear at the balcony of the Imperial Palace several times a day to be greeted by flag-waving crowds which pack the grounds at regular intervals.

15 JANUARY—COMING OF AGE DAY

Young men and women who have celebrated their twentieth birthday in the last twelve months are entertained by parents, schools and employers. They will often be dressed in traditional Japanese costume as they visit a shrine with their family, followed by a nice meal. Employers may give gifts to mark the occasion.

3 OR 4 FEBRUARY—*SETSUBUN*

This marks the end of the winter season and is observed by bean throwing (*mame-maki*) to drive away the devil and ensure good luck for the year. Men born under the animal sign for that year are selected to undertake the throwing of roasted beans at temples and shrines. Occasionally companies may have their own individual bean-throwing ceremonies.

11 FEBRUARY—NATIONAL FOUNDATION DAY

This is a public holiday to commemorate the official founding of the nation but there seemed to be few visible festivities, apart from a few speeches by politicians.

14 FEBRUARY—VALENTINE'S DAY

This is not a public holiday but in recent years seems to have turned into an excuse for exchanging gifts. Unlike Western tradition, it is women who give chocolates to the men. It is estimated that turnover is A$440 million on St Valentine's Day, which represents 10 per cent of all annual sales from chocolate.

3 AND 4 MARCH—*DARUMA ICHI*

The *daruma* doll is a papier-mâché figure which is considered a charm in nearly all small businesses. It reminds me a bit of Humpty Dumpty—a bright red, egg-like shape with no arms or legs. It will always return to an upright position if tipped over. At the time of purchase, the owner paints one eye black to ignite the magical powers. The other eye is only painted when the doll is seen to produce some sort of luck during the year. *Daruma*s are replaced each year and the old ones are ceremoniously burned in temples. They come in a variety of sizes and are often in full view at business sites.

14 MARCH—WHITE DAY

As strange as it may seem, this day is designated for men to give women underwear. It only dates back to the early 1980s and was promoted shamelessly by manufacturers of women's underwear. The theory is that men who received chocolate from women on Valentine's Day may like to reciprocate with a romantic gift and what could be more romantic than underwear? In 1989, about half a million pairs of panties changed hands. Feminists are naturally opposed to the idea but it seems that commercialism prevails. I certainly wouldn't recommend the exchange of such gifts in a business organisation, as the potential for misunderstanding is obvious.

21 MARCH—EQUINOX DAY

There are no obvious celebrations—simply a day off.

APRIL—CHERRY BLOSSOM

Japan is well known for its magnificent cherry blossoms. Tourists and locals alike delight to see the dawning of spring as the landscape is covered with beautiful pink flora. The precise time of the cherry blossom season is dependent on the whims of nature but usually occurs sometime in April.

It is a time for rejoicing as groups of workers are seen gathered under the foliage of the trees. They sing songs and share a drink and a hope for good times ahead; a hope symbolised by the budding blossom.

29 APRIL–5 MAY—GOLDEN WEEK

This is one of the most popular holidays in Japan because many special days are grouped together which allows time for workers to travel without using much annual leave. Many firms and factories will actually close down during this period.

29 APRIL—GREENERY DAY

This was the date of the birthday of Emperor Hirohito, who recently passed away. It is now celebrated as Greenery Day and another holiday has been added to the calendar to mark the birth of the new emperor.

If all subsequent Emperors' birthdays become public holidays, the Japanese will be eventually having more days off work, which theoretically should give the rest of the world a chance to catch up with their impressive productivity levels!

1 MAY—MAY DAY

This is similar to Labour Day in other countries and pays tribute to the average worker.

3 MAY—CONSTITUTION DAY

As the name suggests, this is to mark the founding of the constitution.

MID-JULY—*OBON*

Obon occurs on a weekend in the middle of July. It is not an official holiday but is a time when people are expected to return to their hometowns to pay respect to their ancestors. Trains are packed to capacity and roads clogged with worse than usual traffic jams.

Banks, schools, factories, offices and virtually any other facility which would normally be open on a Saturday or Sunday are closed on this non-official, yet major, occasion. The exceptions are recreational and retail outlets.

15 SEPTEMBER—RESPECT FOR THE AGED DAY

There are no official celebrations for this public holiday which is, as the name suggests, intended to pay respect to senior citizens.

24 SEPTEMBER—AUTUMN EQUINOX

Again, there are no official celebrations for this public holiday.

10 OCTOBER—PHYSICAL CULTURE DAY

Apart from some demonstrations of sport, and media coverage of health promotions, there are no official celebrations for this public holiday.

31 OCTOBER—HALLOWE'EN

The Japanese do not celebrate Hallowe'en or Thanksgiving. However, many merchants have seized upon the time as a marketing opportunity. The larger department stores have elaborate in-store promotions for these occasions. It is surprising to see shelves stocked with appropriate products for Westerners and Western-minded Japanese to consume.

3 NOVEMBER—CULTURE DAY

This is another public holiday with no particular major celebration.

15 NOVEMBER—CHILDREN'S DAY

This is to acknowledge the love for children who have turned three, five or seven during the year. They are often taken to temples and stroll along main streets in traditional costume, looking very cute.

23 NOVEMBER—LABOUR THANKSGIVING DAY

This is another public holiday with no particular major celebration.

DECEMBER
'Tis the season to be jolly . . . because it is the time when workers receive their half-yearly bonus. Unlike the June bonus, a substantial proportion of the December bonus is spent on presents for others.

O-seibo is an old custom whereby you give gifts to those to whom you are indebted for services throughout the year (superiors at companies, teachers, doctors, servants). Shopkeepers usually give small calendars or towels whereas larger companies give more substantial gifts like watches or liquor to valuable customers.

23 DECEMBER—EMPEROR'S BIRTHDAY
This is a recent addition to the Japanese holiday calendar to mark the birthday of the new emperor. Because of the newness, there are no traditional celebrations.

25 DECEMBER—CHRISTMAS DAY
Don't be surprised if Christmas Day is a working day because Japan is not a Christian country and Christmas is not a public holiday. It is becoming somewhat more Westernised in this regard and most multinational companies will also grant employees that day off. But companies are more likely to close for about a week during the New Year period. Christmas is becoming a more popular event in Japan. Although I have no statistics on whether there is a corresponding growth in that religion, I suspect the reason for celebration relates more to taking advantage of a commercial opportunity!

Many expatriates will expect Christmas Day, Easter and Thanksgiving to be public holidays and complain to management that their religion dictates they should not work on those days. Ideally, there should be some scope for flexibility but those expatriates who are likely to express a strong opinion in this regard are usually the same ones who would not wish to trade any of the Japanese holidays.

Management needs to balance between what is fair to all individuals within the work force and decide whether it is productive to have some split holidays.

I believe it is grossly unfair to give expatriates their own religious holidays *and* the Japanese ones. It is equally unproductive to give the entire work force Japanese *and* Western holidays. It would seem logical that on a couple of occasions like Christmas Day and Good Friday, a Westerner might elect to work a day in lieu of a Japanese holiday. However, this is assuming that the Japanese workplace is, in fact, open on that holiday and the person is able to do productive work in isolation from absent colleagues. Although flexibility is ideal, it may not be feasible, so when in Rome do as the Romans do.

LATE DECEMBER—*BONAN KAI*

Bonan Kai is not an official holiday but is the end of the year party where everyone in the workplace gets together to have fun. It is a very informal atmosphere with much alcohol consumed as everyone attempts to erase any bad feelings of the past and look to the future. It seems little different to many Western office Christmas parties, where people try to be super friendly, occasionally disgusting and often regretful of their actions the next day.

Refer also to: Bonus, Gift giving, Parties, Work ethic

HYGIENE FACTORS

I won't cover the entire range of what are commonly termed hygiene factors in human resource management but simply focus on a few observations unique to Japan.

Much has been written about the high standard of working conditions in factories, which may even provide child care and gymnasiums for employees. This is no doubt true of the model companies which we have come to admire in the West. However such standards are far from universal.

Sony, which is undoubtedly one of Japan's true success stories, attributes some of that prosperity to the fact that they chose to air-condition the factories *before* installing it in the offices. It wasn't seen as a status symbol for white-collar workers but rather a practical way to increase the comfort and productivity of the more physically active blue-collar workers.

The humidity in Japan is intense in summer. Most companies issue summer dress codes to make life more bearable for the employee. For example, men are allowed to wear short-sleeved shirts without a tie. This is usually the case whether the office itself is air-conditioned or not because consideration is given to the comfort of the worker while in transit to the workplace. One can well imagine what hygiene factors could be like in the crowded, rush hour subways. There are more people in Tokyo than all of Australia, who all seemed to get on the same train as me every morning, yet there was seldom evidence of body odour.

My experience with standard office accommodation in Japan was draconian. Certainly, there are modern offices with the equivalent of a Western working environment; but a visit to the visa or motor registration office is reminiscent of a trip to a rabbit warren. Desks are crammed close together, air-conditioning absent, files strewn all over the floor and the noise level borders on deafening. Architects would term the layout as open space but there seems very little actual space.

Don't ask for a private office if you're an employee of a Japanese firm. They are few and far between and only the highest-ranking executives warrant them. This is largely because of space limitations but also because of the corporate culture which dictates teams should work together in an open area, rather than have any secrets behind closed doors.

To save money on expensive office space, IBM Japan (which has generous work-space conditions compared to many other companies) introduced a system that squeezes 5000 employees into desk space for only 4500. Every time a sales representative arrives at the office, they check a computer screen to determine what desk is empty. They then wheel their own personal filing cabinet to that space. When they leave to make a sales call, they take the filing cabinet back to a storage area. IBM Japan estimates this will cut its real estate bill by 30 per cent.

Some large Japanese companies provide dormitory accommodation for young trainees. In these instances, all domestic needs would be tended to by the company and most meals eaten on premises in a team environment.

On the other side of the hygiene factor coin . . . What do the Japanese consider when they are thinking of establishing an overseas office? Labour quality and labour climate are important factors. Education facilities are also critical. Many Japanese are appalled at the poor quality of education in overseas schools. They not only want their children to acquire top skills in mathematics, science and traditional subjects; but also have access to Japanese-run schools in order that they may better assimilate when they return to Japan. The Japanese are also more likely to locate in areas which are friendlier to them.

Refer also to: Accommodation, Allowances and benefits, Grooming, Lifelong employment, Medical, Safety, Toilets, Work ethic

I

IDEAS

It has been said that the Japanese are great at copying things but not noted for original ideas and creativity. This may have been true some years ago but today the paradigm has certainly shifted from imitation to innovation.

Most companies have well ingrained suggestion schemes whereby employees are actively encouraged to offer cost-saving ideas. In return, they may receive a direct percentage of the profits gained as a result of implementing that specific suggestion. Even if this is not the case, workers readily recognise that any contributions to enhanced productivity and profits will ultimately increase their semi-annual bonus.

A large percentage of these suggestions would emanate from groups of employees, rather than individuals. Some employees may become embarrassed if singled out for recognition by their management in front of their peers, due to a sense of modesty and the high emphasis placed on being part of a team in Japan.

Refer also to: Bonus, Decisions, Motivation, Quality, Work ethic

INTERNATIONALISM

The Japanese are just as fascinated with our way of doing things as we are with theirs. The electronic media has contributed greatly to this increased awareness of overseas trends. So has the introduction of Western business, from McDonald's to French designer labels.

Perhaps the ultimate testimony to McDonald's success is the fact that the Japanese Ministry of Education has officially complained that nearly half of the nation's school children are clumsy with chopsticks, because of their addiction to hamburgers! There is a story told of a group of Japanese boy scouts visiting Chicago. 'Oh, they have Macu-donaldos in America also,' they squealed with amazement and delight.

Tokyo's Disneyland regularly attracts more visitors than its California counterpart. It is indeed a cosmopolitan city but there appears to be less readiness to embrace Western management practices as wholeheartedly as consumer goods. This, too, is changing as young Japanese are educated overseas, travel on youth exchanges and read Western magazines. Such exposure of this island nation to the outside world is slowly altering the ways of business and society. Overseas university graduates, returning home, expect similar career opportunities to those promised on United States campuses. They expect to be promoted on merit and become impatient at the prospect of relying on a seniority system for reward.

The Japanese have a knowledge of English which is far better than the average American, British or Australian's comprehension of any other language. Although you cannot assume that English will be understood, there is a good chance that you will find someone with whom you can converse.

The *Japanese Times*, the only English newspaper, attempts to cover news from various countries. They also capitalise on this internationalism and run special features on almost every country's National Day. It used to amuse and irritate me that India's National Day received more coverage than Australia's, which both fall on 26 January. The fact that there are more Indians than Australians in Tokyo (and the world) did little to appease this unjustified logic of mine.

Successful Western companies may do their best to preserve the myth which surrounds doing business with the Japanese. Victor Harris, president of Max Factor's Japanese subsidiary, openly admits, 'I'm not going to help people compete with me. When I talk to groups in the States, I always tell them it's impossible to get into the Japanese market. And I think there's a lot of that.'

If an expatriate manager performs poorly in Japan, the reasons for doing so seem paradoxical. They either try to operate purely on a Western basis, with no understanding or tolerance of local conditions, *or* totally ignore home office by becoming too Japanese, thus losing credibility with their headquarters.

Many multinational Japanese organisations have strategies characterised as global localisation. They think globally and act locally. They take the company's global policies into consideration, regardless of what country they are operating in. At the same time, they closely monitor political, economic and cultural movements to enable them to act in accord with what seems most appropriate in the local marketplace.

Sony has approximately 100 000 employees throughout the world. Approximately 45 per cent of this number work abroad; of which 700 are of Japanese nationality ('A Review of Fosterage and Appointment of Foreign employees', Human Resource Planning Office of Sony, Makoto Fukano).

Personnel managers of the various overseas operating units meet once a year to discuss mutual issues. Tokyo exerts little control over the practices and procedures within the countries, although there are obviously many similarities due to the regular meetings and need to have the same basic principles.

Historically, most Japanese firms operating in other countries have been managed by Japanese. This is still predominantly the case although most firms would espouse the wish to appoint more local people to management positions. The same is true of Western companies with overseas subsidiaries. The theory of appointing locals to senior positions is a sound one. This brings the benefits of familiarity with the country and culture. It demonstrates good corporate citizenship by creating employment opportunities within that country. And, most significantly, there is the obvious reduced cost of not having to pay an expatriate salaries and allowances if locals are appointed.

Anyone wishing to pursue an international career with Sony must be able to speak English. Sony, Mitsui and many other Japanese firms now recruit graduates from overseas universities to join the local staff and progress through the company. Any non-graduate who is serious about climbing the corporate ladder should also learn Japanese. Can you imagine someone becoming chairman of General Motors if they couldn't speak English?

It is no secret that the Japanese are rapidly expanding their worldwide investments. Front page headlines are made when they purchase national landmarks like Rockefeller Center in New York, prestige hotels in London and golf resorts in Australia. Their presence is also growing in Europe. In the fiscal year ending 31 March 1990, Japanese companies put US$ 14.4 billion into direct investments in Europe; which was a 74 per cent increase over the previous year. (*Fortune* magazine, 2 July 1990, p. 27).

The Japanese are placing particular focus on the eastern bloc countries in the hope of creating yet another economic miracle. They are even advising the Soviets on the establishment of a stock exchange and are very active in China, a country they once occupied.

Whether or not traditional Japanese management and personnel practices will work universally as well in societies other than Japan, is yet to be seen. However, the successful companies are unlikely to totally impose their head office practices outside the country; nor wholeheartedly adopt the working culture of the country in which they operate. In other words, they will unknowingly follow the advice that is given in this book to Western companies operating in Japan and . . . *treat situations and individuals uniquely!*

Refer also to: Communication . . . and useful phrases, Lifelong employment, Tradition, X-pats

J

JUNIORS

In the work environment, a junior is almost the same as a joke. They have historically not been treated seriously by their superiors; but as the younger Japanese are more exposed to Western management practices, their expectations are changing.

Refer also to: Seniority, Youth

K

KARAOKE

As a child who was instructed to simply pretend to be a goldfish and mouth the words in the Sunday school choir, the prospect of being required to sing in front of colleagues at a karaoke bar was one of my most daunting experiences in Japan.

Here are a few tips for others who may not possess the musical talents of Joan Sutherland or Billy Joel . . .

Intimidation rapidly turns to terror as the first person to volunteer is usually a terrific tenor who loves the limelight. One keeps hoping you will be overlooked as the Japanese revel in this strange camaraderie but it is inevitable you will be called upon for a rendition of some sort. Participation is not optional! The trick is to first admit that you can't sing but nevertheless give it a go. You will be surprised at how even the worst voices bear some resemblance to a harmonic tune with the aid of echo microphones and an enthusiastic audience. Try to wait until later in the evening when the group is somewhat more lubricated by alcohol to be overly critical of your vocal chords.

Laser disks may be provided with words written in English. You will most certainly find the words to 'My Way' or 'The Impossible Dream'. If such accompaniment doesn't exist, you'll gain extra brownie points with the audience if you can sing anything in Japanese. However, a quick round of 'Waltzing Matilda' or a Maori rugby call will suffice. The important thing is to participate!

Informality is the norm on these occasions and it is common to see people of high and low rank, arms around each other, swaying and singing together. It's also less embarrassing to volunteer for a duet or quartet.

Refer also to: Entertainment, Parties

L

LEGAL MATTERS

Very simply, remember to abide by the laws of the country in which you are a resident. Criminal offences are similar to any other developed nation. There has been a greater influx of foreign lawyers in recent years but the Japanese are generally more inclined to settle disputes out of court.

Refer also to: Automobiles, Baggage, Death, Medical, Pets, Safety and security, Tax, Visas and other legal documents

LIFELONG EMPLOYMENT

This is the human resource principle for which the Japanese management system is probably best known. It embraces a womb to tomb approach to employment. Until recently, it was most unusual for a worker to voluntarily change jobs.

However, contrary to public opinion, the concept of lifelong employment has never been a universal practice in Japan. It was often limited to men and many women were asked to leave an organisation when they married. Lifelong employment was much more prevalent in government and large corporations. Such bodies traditionally saw themselves as social, as well as economic, institutions, and actively promoted the concept of the company as a family unit. Lifelong employment has never been the norm in smaller enterprises, which are not always able to afford the overheads of keeping staff during bad economic times.

In fact, according to Haruo Shimada, professor of economics at Keio University, only about 25 per cent of employees are really a part of the full lifetime employment and seniority system of wages. In a paper delivered to the Industrial Relations Seminar at Massachusetts Institute of Technology in 1982, he goes on to state that 10–20 per cent of employees leave firms every year. Turnover rates are higher for females than males, and higher for smaller companies than larger ones. According to his figures, half of newly hired people each year are those who have occupational experience somewhere else. This has become even more prevalent in the last ten years.

Firms are wary of hiring large numbers of staff in times of boom. They are sensitive to the longer term social implications if it becomes necessary to initiate lay-offs because of a downturn in business. That is why you will often find large numbers of temporary staff being utilised. Some of these so-called temps may have worked at the company for years but have never been given the expectation, and affiliated commitment and benefits, which accompany full-time employment.

The depression of 1975 saw significant changes to the concept of lifelong employment. There was an increase in the number of free workers who were paid by the work they did. These were usually part-time workers or those who shared a job. There was no obligation by the employer to pay regular increases or promote by seniority.

Most Japanese companies hire young graduates and promote people to senior ranks from within the same company. This practice of 'grow your own' executives is still very prevalent in Japan and it is unusual for an outsider to be head-hunted to fill a management position.

However, as Japan becomes more Westernised, the trend is towards changing jobs. This is evidenced by the number of head-hunting firms that have successfully established offices in Tokyo in recent times. The number of such firms is estimated to have risen from 50 to 250 in the last five years!

It is also estimated that Japanese head-hunters control about 90 per cent of the business, but the influx of international firms is now receiving an increasing slice of the market share. At first, these organisations were viewed with suspicion. Those who dealt with them were also seen in an unfavourable light because of the historical stigma that they had not met the obligations to the company which originally hired them.

Increasing internationalism and the quest, particularly for Japanese with skills in their own field plus language abilities, has made this a new ball game.

In a recent survey, a record 38.5 per cent of Japanese managers between 20 and 39 said they were thinking of changing jobs. 'When the boss of a Tokyo software company opened the door of his design department a few months ago, he found the room deserted. The entire department had been recruited by a rival company' (*Fortune* magazine, 21 May, 1990, p. 38).

Setsuka Egami, editor of a Tokyo job placement magazine, states:

> The virtue of work used to be its own reward. Now the virtue of work is money. This doesn't mean that Japanese aren't continuing to work hard and produce good work. They do. They just don't bother about which company as much.

Again, do not overgeneralise with the statement that all Japanese are now more willing to change jobs. Takashi Kurisaka, a partner at Egon Zehnder, the third-largest executive company in the world, says: 'People are still brand-conscious. Joining Mitsubishi bank provides social prestige. I've heard people say they will consider a switch after they marry off their daughter' (*Fortune* magazine, 21

May, 1990, p. 38).

Because of the practice of lifetime employment in large companies, workers do not feel threatened by the introduction of new technology which will increase productivity by reducing actual manpower. Quite the contrary . . . because their bonuses are linked to the overall profit of the company, they embrace technological change, rather than go on strike for fear of retrenchment.

Changes in worker expectations have resulted in re-evaluating Japan's lifelong employment system. In response to such changes, Ricoh, a large electronics company, began a unique career-planning practice in 1978. In this new arrangement, promotions are stopped temporarily when the employee reaches 35 years of age. Each employee is asked to re-examine whether their position in the company meets their personal needs and life philosophy. When they reach 40, they should have a very clear idea of whether they should remain with the company or seek other employment more suitable to their desires. Other companies have begun to look at similar situations but instances are rather isolated. It is certainly not common for an employee in mid to late thirties to change a company as a result of such an examination of their life, simply because it is still unusual for other companies to hire persons of that age.

In spite of the recent economic downturn, Japan still has one of the lowest unemployment rates in the world. It also has the highest ratio of 'middlemen' in the world and, in spite of excellent technology, there are always enough jobs for the workers. A prime example is on the ski slopes. You are given electronically encoded lift passes which would theoretically allow you simply to insert them in a card reader to gain access to the lift gate. However, there is usually one person to take your card and put it in the electronic reader, another to help you on the chair and a third who stands around to supervise that this activity progresses smoothly.

In terms of product distribution, there is not simply a supplier, wholesaler and retailer. In some cases, there may be a couple of wholesalers in the distribution chain. Naturally, this all contributes to the high cost of goods but ensures minimal unemployment.

There are few outside board members. Most organisations choose to draw their membership from within the ranks. The notable exceptions are those men (and most *are* men) who are longstanding executives of affiliate companies, or companies with which an organisation has a strong business dependency or relationship. It is very common for companies to have a member of their bank on the board. It is also quite normal practice for a company to employ a person who has retired from another subsidiary company. For example, someone who was a senior executive with Mitsubishi Bank may retire and become a senior executive with Mitsubishi Automotive.

Nearly every company in the world pays lip service to the statement that employees are the most valuable asset. But only those who look after employees in tough economic times bring any credibility to that statement! In Japan, the notion of lifelong employment is not just window dressing. Likewise, IBM had a similar philosophy and until recently had never laid anyone off due to a management consultant commenting that IBM is more Japanese than Western in its management style.

Refer also to: Education and training, Hygiene factors, Obligation, Recruiting, Resignation and retrenchment, Retirement, Seniority, Temporaries, Transfers, Work ethic

LOTTERIES

Lotteries proved a constant source of amazement to me in Japan. I'm not simply talking about buying a lottery ticket for a prize draw but the use of lotteries in some day to day transactions. Rather than operate purely on the law of supply and demand or first come, first serve, one would often obtain tickets to popular rock concerts or even a speech by Mother Teresa via a lottery! If you want to book tennis courts at a local council, there are lotteries held once a month for the few available times.

Lotteries are seen as a very fair thing. Even purchases of popular apartments may be done by chance, rather than to the highest bidder. I remember visiting a Japanese friend who proudly told me about the multimillion yen purchase of his three-bedroom apartment. 'We were very lucky. We wanted an apartment on the top floor (which was more prestigious and expensive) but we were lucky to be able to win a chance to buy a less expensive one on the seventh floor.'

In this particular complex, there were over 20 bidders for every unit. Prospective purchasers were requested to pay a sizeable deposit up front to demonstrate their serious intentions. Those who were unsuccessful received refunds.

Refer also to: Allowances and benefits, Sport and recreation

LUNCHES

The lunch hour starts early in Japan and workers begin their midday meal around 11.30 a.m. This is because many of them have left home very early in order to commute to work. There are always two or three luncheon sittings at local restaurants. Set-course lunches are the norm and much cheaper than ordering à la carte.

The 'long lunch' is not usual business format and entertainment of clients tends to be reserved for the evening. Again, this can vary when hosting overseas visitors.

Refer also to: Entertainment, Food

M

MEDIA

There are a number of English-language newspapers readily available in Tokyo. This is not the case in more remote areas. Tokyo residents can also readily avail themselves of international newspapers such as the *Asian Wall Street Journal* and *USA Today*.

A couple of free magazines written in English are also available from supermarkets and major hotels. These provide details of current happenings in Tokyo as well as a range of advertising which can actually be quite useful to the foreigner. Other publications written in English and other foreign languages are available by subscription and the consulate of your home country could provide you with information on access to these.

There are a number of radio stations which provide access to popular and classical music but the dialogue is all in Japanese. The exception is the armed forces network, which is in English and is useful for news and weather reports. Access to international services, such as the BBC, are possible if you have a powerful shortband radio.

Television is all in Japanese, except for some large hotels and apartments which offer cable. Even if you never turn on your television and only use it to play English-speaking videos, you are still meant to pay a television tax which is collected by someone who comes to your door.

Refer also to: Miscellaneous

MEDICAL

Medical care is always of concern in a strange environment. Even though Tokyo has excellent English-speaking doctors and dentists, and hospitals which have access to English, there are some things you should be particularly aware of.

I believe all expatriates should be required to have a comprehensive medical examination before accepting an assignment. There is enough stress associated with living in a foreign culture without the need to worry about pre-existing medical conditions. It could also save employers considerable amounts of money. If an employee is insecure about being treated in a foreign land, it is risky to send them in the first place as it is very expensive and non-productive to fly them home for treatment.

Ensure you have adequate health insurance, as treatment is very expensive. Payment may be demanded in cash, since cheques are not a usual means of paying for services.

It is strongly recommended, within a few days of arrival, to make a preliminary visit to a doctor *before* any emergency occurs. You will have a million and one things to do when you first arrive and will probably not want to worry about a problem you don't yet have. However, I can't emphasise how important it is to take a bit of time to feel comfortable with arrangements, should you require medical treatment. Check with your embassy for a reputable doctor near you who speaks your language.

There is a very useful service in Tokyo called TELL–Tokyo

English Life Line. They are staffed 9.00 a.m.–1.00 p.m. and 7.00 p.m.–midnight. Their key role is to assist with translation in emergencies but they also provide counselling to distressed expatriates. This service is only available in Tokyo and you cannot guarantee you will become sick during those hours, so always carry in your wallet, in two languages, the name of your doctor and a contact number for a bilingual friend in case of an emergency.

Refer also to: Death

MEETINGS

One only needs to attend a couple of meetings in Japan to discover that the Japanese are not as efficient with time as they are with space! Many people are present but relatively few participate. There seems to be no set time limit to the duration of the meeting. Not all meetings are long-drawn-out affairs which don't seem to reach a conclusive decision—only most of them!

Nema washi is the name given to the process of getting together with other players before the meeting starts to obtain consensus on certain issues through the informal process. It is essentially lobbying and much of it is conducted outside the office in a social environment. The meeting then becomes a formalisation of many decisions already reached.

Punctuality is highly valued in all aspects of life. Even at a memorial service in Hiroshima, over 60 000 people commenced the ceremony promptly at 8.15 a.m. It would be incredibly bad form to arrive late for a business meeting. Even legitimate excuses of being caught in Tokyo traffic will not suffice, so plan to reach your destination well in advance of the scheduled time. Don't be surprised if Japanese associates arrive early and expect you to drop everything.

The best way to establish business contacts is to be formally introduced by a mutual acquaintance; preferably in person but a letter of introduction will also be useful.

Most loan applications still require an introduction to a banker by a person willing to act as guarantor.

Generally speaking, the business code still dictates that only a president of one company meet with a president of another, a senior manager with a senior manager etc. However, the rules on this are somewhat open to interpretation and there is no particular obligation for the president of Honda to meet with the president of a ten person operation.

At any meeting, there will inevitably be more people present than those required to make the decision. Individuals will contribute to the discussion to varying degrees. Don't be dreadfully offended if someone has their eyes closed during the meeting. They are likely to be still somewhat alert—a skill developed by dozing on the train and somehow miraculously managing to alight at the correct station. However, if a few people are showing a lack of interest, you may wish to change tack.

The person who does most of the talking may not necessarily be the decision maker. In fact, there may be no single decision maker, so it is important to address your comments to all present.

Allow plenty of time to wind up a meeting. Do not continually look at your watch impatiently, nor end the meeting abruptly. You can subtly indicate you are ready to leave by collecting your papers. It is considered very poor manners to rush off, because it implies that the party you are meeting with is not as important as the one you are about to see.

However, if you are on a tight schedule during a limited visit to Japan, you can indicate to your host at the time the meeting is first arranged that you will need to be elsewhere at an appointed hour.

Do not try to fit too many meetings into a short space of time and always allow substantially more time than you think would be necessary. For example, if you arrange to meet between 10.00 a.m. and 12.00 p.m., you should not plan another appointment until 2.00 p.m. Be prepared to return for future discussions, as the first meeting may be seen as little more than a courtesy call. At one stage, the first meeting *was* only that but this is also changing as Japanese businesspeople increasingly focus on their time as an asset.

In Japan, there is no question that meetings can be even more frustrating than normal. The bad news is that it does, indeed, take a longer time to reach consensus. The good news is that once agreement is finally achieved, the implementation process is not so arduous. This is the key difference from decision making as we know it. In the West, participants are usually eager to appear helpful and enthusiastic to an initial idea. They make all the right noises which indicate they will proceed. It often occurs, following agreement in principle, that obstacles appear which prevent ultimate implementation of the proposal. In Japan, the original position is one of caution, not enthusiasm. From that position, there is less room for disappointment arising from raising high expectations.

Refer also to: Bowing, Business cards, Communication . . . and useful phrases, Decisions, Discretion . . . and loss of face, Ideas, Names, Patience, Seniority, Work ethic, Yes

MISCELLANEOUS

This is a collection of useful and interesting information which doesn't neatly fit into any other category.

* Walk on the left hand side of the street and don't jump queues in shops or public transport.
* Statistics are a way of life in Japanese organisations. Great pride is taken in quantitatively analysing even the most trivial piece of information in hopes that it may reveal some useful trend.
* Never assume anything! I once sat through a Chinese film with Japanese subtitles. The photography was great but I gleaned little of the plot. Yet, the amazing thing was that it had been advertised in English!
* The annual peace ceremony to commemorate the bombing of Hiroshima is also in Japanese. I was one of the few Westerners who attended with 60 000 locals. I didn't need to understand the language to comprehend the emotion. The crowd was overwhelmingly friendly and I couldn't help but wonder if a Japanese visitor would receive as warm a welcome if they casually strolled into an Anzac ceremony in Australia or Legion memorial in the United States.
* Newspaper headlines never ceased to amaze me although a closer examination of our own media would no doubt reveal similar bemusement to an overseas visitor. Through the press, we were kept informed of such earth-shattering events as:

—Koalas in the local zoo were suffering from bladder infection.

—The prime minister discussing his diet—political and intestinal.

—During 1987, 39 employees of Japan Rail committed suicide, apparently as a result of anxiety surrounding the privatisation of the operation.

—A Buddhist priest blessing 70 000 used brassieres heaped in a pyramid, at a memorial service for cast-off underwear. This actually proved a successful promotional stunt for a lingerie firm.

As I said, the Western press can be just as sensationalised but I found these instances particularly bemusing and they may, just *may*, shed some light on the human nature of the country.

MOTIVATION

There is absolutely no correlation between meetings and motivation!

Refer also to: Allowances and benefits, Hygiene factors, Recruiting, Salary, Work ethic

N

NAMES

My biggest fear when I first stepped into the Tokyo office was that everyone not only seemed to look the same, but their names all sounded identical to my ignorant ear. Don't be intimidated by this and you will soon discover that people do not look, sound or think the same!

Admit that it's not going to be easy to learn unfamiliar sounds but make a conscious effort to pronounce names. People understand if you make mistakes but not if you don't make an effort! After a few stumbles and giggles, your ear becomes more attuned to the different syllables.

Remember, we are all individuals and our name is one of the most personal things we possess. We expect the respect it brings. You would never think of doing business in the West without learning Charlie McGuinness's or Marion Bartholomew's name. So why, in Japan, would some Westerners have the audacity to ask if they could shorten a Japanese name to one which is more easily pronounceable?

I know of one instance where an American, when meeting a man called Sumitomo for the first time, said, 'I'll never remember all that so I'll just call you Sam'. That's somewhat different from an instance in which a Japanese acquaintance might say, 'Just call me Matt because Westerners can never say Matsumoto'. How you chose to address that individual then becomes a matter of individual preference and judgement. It is not a lot different from a Westerner whose name is Catherine saying 'Most people call me Cathy'. The fact is that close friends call me Cath but I would be somewhat offended if anyone took the liberty to shorten it further to 'Cat'.

If I'm not sure if an individual actually prefers to be called by their full name and is only compromising because they feel I can't pronounce it, I will state that I am certainly able to address them by their full name and ask what they prefer. Believe me, after a few weeks of concerted effort, you will easily be able to discern the differences between Ushiyama and Ishiyama, Kanamaru and Kawamura. And you will be a lot closer to building a solid business rapport and long term relationship.

It is customary to call someone by their surname, with a *san* tacked on the end. Therefore, you would refer to Mr or Ms Smith as Smith-*san*. Some may ask that you call them by their first names. That is perfectly acceptable but unless they make a point of it, you should always give them the respect by the *san* title.

Expatriates don't need to be fluent in Japanese (although it helps). They *do* need to be the sort of person who will make an effort to learn a person's name. No one likes to be referred to as 'hey you' or 'the guy who looks after salaries'. If you perceive this occurring in your company, don't give expatriates any excuse. Put up an organisational chart in a public place with names, titles and photos next to each position. I couldn't believe the increase in morale and efficiency when I did this. The Japanese staff responded positively to being treated as individuals and expatriates no longer felt compelled to immediately come to me as a Westerner for any issue they had.

Some men may take the surname of their in-laws in instances where the wife's family doesn't have any sons. By taking the family name, her husband is also entitled to the family assets.

Refer also to: Business cards, Communication . . . and useful phrases, Discretion . . . and loss of face

O

OBLIGATION

This is the 'big O' and there are a multitude of obligations in Japanese society. In short, if someone does you a favour, you are indebted to them. Therefore, people may be reluctant to offer help as they don't wish to embarrass someone by implied obligation.

I learned a little more about obligation when I returned a wallet which I found on a rural train. I handed it to the conductor, who had another passenger verify the amount of money as approximately US$400. We were both required to fill in detailed forms. It seemed to take an inordinate amount of time and I was so worried about missing my next connection that I never gave the matter another thought. I was surprised when the railway phoned me a few days later to inform me they had located the owner. Many years later, I still receive letters of thanks from him. I had to refuse numerous offers of presents for what I considered a basic act of honesty. He considered it an obligation.

I found that politeness often reached extremes between people who know each other. Such consideration is far from evident in the jostling which occurs in crowded subways. This is very simply because you have no obligation if you have not formally been introduced. Therefore, the masses do not warrant the same consideration as acquaintances.

Nevertheless, I still found the Japanese extraordinarily

helpful to total strangers. Someone would inevitably stop to ask if you required directions and more often than not go out of their own way to personally escort you to your destination. Although they expect nothing for this courtesy, Westerners would do well to remember that there is still an underlying sense of implied obligation; even if this means nothing more than providing them with the opportunity to practise their English while you are together.

Obligation in Japan is a world of *On, Gimu* and *Giri*. *On* refers to the indebtedness an individual automatically inherits merely by being born or through marriage. *Gimu* represents the unconditional and unceasing obligations due to parents and country. *Giri* is the hardest to bear and most difficult to define. It can consist of a wide array of repayments to family members, colleagues, employers, friends and one's own honour.

Within a business environment, obligation works both ways. The worker has an obligation to the boss and the company and vice versa.

There is a saying *Giray Choko* which describes such acts as giving a New Year's card to your boss, even if you don't like the person. This is an obligation because other co-workers will do so and you would not want to be seen as less enthusiastic. No Japanese would confirm that this equated to what we would term 'brown-nosing', probably because it would be impossible to translate in polite terms, but I think *Giray Choko* is much the same thing.

A few years ago, a Japan Airlines plane crashed, killing over 500 passengers. The chairman of the company resigned. In Japan, such an action is not only appropriate, but obligatory. Even now, newspapers report that over 200 relatives still attend memorial services at the mountain site for those victims killed in the 1985 crash. The ceremony is also attended by about 20 executives of Japan Airlines, including the new president, who renew their pledge not to repeat such a disaster.

In 1987, the chairman of Toshiba resigned when the US government prohibited imports of Toshiba products because of the company's role in sales of restricted machinery to the USSR. Here was an instance of the most senior executive taking the blame, even though the sales were made through a junior subsidiary company without his knowledge. This sort of executive action certainly brings renewed meaning to the phrase 'the buck stops here'.

In such a guilt-ridden society, it is not surprising that suicide is still regarded as the ultimate apology, rather than suffering shame.

You often see workers practising their golf swing with imaginary clubs at train and bus stops. One man was swinging an actual club in a narrow street when he accidentally hit and killed a passerby on a bicycle. Although no charges were laid, the golfer resigned from his job and paid all his retirement benefits to the bereaved family. In spite of this, the deceased woman's husband complained to the media that the man's company had extended no formal apology to him for allowing an employee to swing a golf club in a congested area.

I probably never did fully understand my obligations as a manager. I had read that it used to be obligatory for a manager to act as a go-between and arrange marriages for staff. Although I realised it certainly wasn't a prerequisite in the 1990s, I thought I might gain kudos by lining up my secretary with a nice young geography teacher. I was, admittedly, a little disappointed that they didn't seem to have even a flicker of romance. However, young Japanese are quite willing and able to make their own choices by meeting other young people who share similar interests. Unknown to me, my secretary had been seeing another young man, whom she later brought to Australia on their honeymoon. We laughed about the fact that she had only dated the geography teacher out of obligation to me for making the arrangement! Here was a classic case of both parties trying to meet traditional obligations when a little open communication would have prevented such a farce.

Refer also to: Discretion . . . and loss of face, Entertainment, Gift giving, Lifelong employment, Safety and security, Visas

P

PARTIES

Everyone loves a party and the Japanese are no exception. Social get togethers provide everyone with an opportunity to let their hair down. The good news is that words spoken under the influence of alcohol are conveniently forgotten the next day by all parties at the party.

In fact, the *bonankai* is the end of year office party with the express purpose of getting together, airing grievances and then completely disregarding all past differences, in order to make a clean start on the new year. There may be parties associated with various other holiday seasons throughout the year.

Office parties are usually centred around the opening of a new branch, celebrating a particular achievement or *sayonara* for a retiring employee or expatriate returning home. On all occasions, one should be prepared for an early start and finish. They are generally buffet format and everyone makes a dash for the table after their tummies have rumbled through a myriad of speeches. This is often followed by seemingly endless choruses of singing known as Karioke.

Speaking of preparedness . . . never go to a party without an abundance of easily accessible business cards.

Some large office parties have receiving lines to enable the key executives to meet with each customer or employee. It is not unusual to receive a gift when you leave this sort of party.

Big corporations may go to great extremes to have elaborate celebrations for major events. In commemoration of its fiftieth anniversary, IBM Japan hired Tokyo Disneyland to express appreciation for the company's success to the 20 000 staff and families. I was enthusiastically recounting the fun and commenting on how unique IBM was in this regard, only to be informed that other large companies did likewise.

Obviously, the majority of businesses wouldn't have the critical mass to hire Disneyland but that wouldn't prevent employees from XYZ enjoying themselves with colleagues.

I had the good fortune to attend the Christmas party of employees from the Oshima Water Board, a small still-active volcanic island of only 10 000 inhabitants. It seemed strange to eat raw fish for Christmas dinner but stranger still that not one attendee was Christian. However, that did not deter them from singing Christmas carols, having the boss dress up as Santa and exchanging colourfully wrapped gifts via a game similar to musical chairs. The men dressed up as women, played silly party games, consumed copious quantities of food and alcohol, danced, sang and took photographs all night. And there were only a dozen of them.

So, don't tell me Japanese are staid!

Refer also to: Bowing, Business cards, Communication . . . and useful phrases, Education and training, Entertainment, Food, Holidays and festivals, Karaoke

PATIENCE

Patience is something which every Westerner needs in abundance when dealing with the Japanese, or any foreign culture, for that matter. You must accept that you are an outsider and there is an inevitable learning curve. Everything takes longer to do than in your familiar home territory. No one ever said it would be easy.

The Japanese respect persistence so:

- If at first you don't succeed, keep on trying.
- Be patient.
- Hang in there.

I could add a few more cliches to this list but the truth is that I feel totally inadequate to give authoritative advice on this subject. I was surely at the back of the queue when patience was being handed out. When I told friends I was going to Japan on a two year assignment, they chuckled that it must be divine retribution for my lack of patience. They hoped I would 'learn' that virtue. I'm not sure if I ever did but at least I did *try*.

Refer also to: Everything you do in Japan! But, particularly to entries on Banking, Communication . . . and useful phrases, Decisions, Discretion . . . and loss of face, Lifelong employment, Meetings, Obligation, Tradition, Work ethic, Yes

PETS

There are certain regulations regarding taking pets to Japan. These are not particularly stringent and usually only involve simple inoculations and filling in the appropriate form to register your pet as 'unaccompanied baggage'. A greater difficulty may arise in the quarantine restrictions of a pet returning to a country like Australia. Be sure to check before you leave home.

The decision whether or not to take a pet is a personal one and depends on the length of stay, amount of travel away from home, type of accommodation and breed of animal. Because I was only going to stay in Japan for a maximum of two years, and Australian authorities at the time required nine months in quarantine for my dog to return to Australia, I decided it would not be fair at her age to be in kennels for that length of time. As much as I adore my dog, I reluctantly recognised that Tokyo is not a pet-friendly city. Make sure you are conscious of the needs of the animal . . . not just your own selfish wants to have them with you in a very urban environment.

If you do chose to bring them, they must be vaccinated and registered once a year at the local ward office.

Refer also to: Baggage

POLITICS

This is an intentionally short section as there have been such enormous changes to the political landscape in the last year which would warrant an entire book devoted to the subject for those interested. But, for the average person living in Japan, the party in power is of little relevance. The protocol of exchanging niceties at social functions, inviting politicians to events etc. are much the same as in the West and appropriateness is based on individual circumstances.

Non-Japanese are not allowed to vote but I could never understand why politicians hired vans with multi-decibel megaphones to terrorise unsuspecting neighbourhoods at 8.00 a.m. on Saturday mornings, with campaign promises to reduce noise pollution!

POSTAL

The postal service is as efficient as any in the world. It generally would take 5–10 days for airmail letters to travel between Tokyo and any other major capital city in the world.

There was mail delivery on Saturdays and post offices were open. One post office at the south exit of the Maranouchi Tokyo station was open 24 hours!

If sending large volumes of Christmas cards or change of address notifications, it is considerably cheaper to plan well in advance and send by sea mail and allow 6–8 weeks for delivery.

Parcels mailed overseas must contain a customs declaration of the contents.

There is not a a great deal of difference from Western postal systems except that special envelopes are available to mail cash. This is quite common and apparently reliable.

Refer also to: Baggage

Q

QUALITY

Many excellent books have been entirely devoted to this important subject and it would be less than a 'quality' effort if I even pretended to cover the spectrum in a few paragraphs. Yet, so often we hear the question: 'If the Japanese can consistently produce quality goods, why can't we?'.

The answer is a simple one. We can! Or, I should say, we can *if* we choose to. There is no Japanese secret in this regard. In fact, it was an American by the name of W. Edwards Deming who is credited with introducing the concept of quality circles to Japan, after his ideas had been firmly rejected in the United States.

This was at a time when Japanese products were certainly not regarded as high quality. In fact, anything that bore the label 'Made in Japan' was shunned by consumers. It was considered cheap, imitation junk. The paradigm has changed and Japanese goods are now regarded in exactly the opposite light as expensive, innovative, high quality products.

This is no accident and the Japanese take great pride in the phenomenal progress they have made. I still chuckle at a middle aged factory worker, with little command of English, who pointed to himself and with a broad smile, proudly declared, 'I am good worker. I am also made in Japan'.

Such workers actually meet in their own time to improve the quality of products. This must be partially due to the fact that their salaries and bonuses are linked directly to the success of the company. But this would be too simplistic an explanation in itself. There is a commitment to producing quality goods; a commitment which evolved from the absolute necessity and desire to revive the economy after the War, by whatever means possible. Now that Western economies are nearing a crisis situation, one might hope to see similar levels of improved commitment to quality. No one ever said the path to quality would be easy. It wasn't any easier for the Japanese. It didn't happen overnight but through years of constantly striving for improvement.

In their pursuit of quality, the Japanese have implemented many processes which objectively measure standards to ensure they are getting as close as possible to defect-free. They operate on the principle that 'What gets measured gets done'. This applies not only in traditional manufacturing but in every aspect of the business. Measurements in human resource management would determine such things as: whether a practitioner has zero errors on a form they fill in; if 100 per cent of employees are given salary raises at the appropriate time; if 95 per cent are sent to company orientation programs within a month of joining the firm.

Through worker participation, there is a steady flow of shop-floor suggestions for improvements to products and processes.

Quality is not a simple fix. As already mentioned, there are a number of books available, as well as seminars, which provide a practical framework to implement quality improvement programs.

Refer also to: Bonus, Salary, Service, Unions, Work ethic

R

RECRUITING

Japan's booming economy and rapidly ageing population oncee produced a severe labour shortage. It was estimated that there were currently 140 jobs for every 100 job seekers (*Fortune* magazine, 13 August 1990, p. 9). This, too, is changing but recruiting is still considered very important.

Similar to Western recruiting practice, companies try to entice top graduates by offering attractive compensation and benefits packages. They naturally promote the company as a good place to work and promise encouraging career opportunities. The prospect of business travel is very appealing to young Japanese.

To attract talented young engineers, in a tough labour market, Kawasaki Steel has even resorted to airing a television rock video which portrays the company as a fun place to work.

However, universities still provide the strongest link in the recruitment chain. Employers invest considerable time establishing relationships with leading academics. These professors usually have considerable influence over which firm their top graduates will join. Companies assign alumni ('old boys') of that particular university to build up a close relationship over a number of years with the head of the engineering, business or computer departments. They are often employees who themselves were initially recommended to the firm by an academic as a result of the old-boys' network.

It would not be unusual to see many employees from

one university within the same section of a company. At one point in history, the public service only recruited graduates from Tokyo University and is still noted for the high percentage of graduates from that campus. Stories are told that some outstanding graduates of Tokyo University were so highly recommended by professors they were actually hired without even a job interview. This would not be the norm.

Most students would expect extensive interviews and it is not unusual for a student to have 4–5 interviews. They may even spend a day on site with a potential employer before being offered a job.

There is a recruiting season prior to most new employees joining a company on 1 April of each year. When it is announced certain companies will be visiting campuses, newspapers carry photographs of long queues of students lined up to join the most prestigious companies. Surveys are published in the press every year which analyse those firms which students most wish to join; how that company compared to the previous year; male/female breakdowns etc.

The long-term relationship between a company and a university makes it more difficult for foreign companies which have recently established in Japan to gain access to the best graduates. However, some companies like IBM have been in the recruiting game for many years. Interestingly enough, a survey by a leading economic daily newspaper, *Nihon Keizai Shimbun*, ranked IBM Japan as the best company to work for. The survey quizzed 123 companies on working conditions, benefits, pay and promotion. IBM came out ahead of any other Japanese or multinational firm. It is also ranked as the number one preference among female graduates; which is related to its widely stated equal opportunity policy. This has made it attractive to young women who may see more limited opportunity for advancement within the more established Japanese organisations.

In spite of this, it is not easy for every new or foreign company to recruit experienced and skilled personnel. This is partially related to lifelong employment and the former reluctance of employees to change jobs. But it is also indicative of a reluctance to join an organisation without a firmly established track record. Foreign companies who are involved in a joint venture will often have their Japanese partner offer to supply key personnel. This can be very useful but foreign firms should be careful they are not saddled with management who are no longer considered capable of performing in the mainstream of the parent company.

Most new employees are put on probation for an average period of six months. After a successful probation period, they are welcomed into the office at a small party and presented with a gift or some other token of their successful initiation into the 'family'.

The chairman of Sony introduced a unique policy of disregarding academic records once someone was hired. This was to ensure that employees were judged on their actual performance at work and their supervisor was not swayed either positively or negatively by professorial comments on their scholastic ability.

Specific reference to head-hunting is included in Lifelong employment. Refer also to: Allowances and benefits, Hygiene factors, Lifelong employment, Obligation, Salary, Youth

RESIGNATION AND RETRENCHMENT

Companies place great emphasis on careful recruiting because they hope that an employee will stay with them for life.

In spite of the recession, it is still not common practice to fire someone in Japan. However, if tough economic times force major cutbacks in the work force, the pattern usually adopted is:

- freeze on hiring;
- freeze on overtime work;
- release those on short term contracts;
- managers take a salary cut;
- older workers farmed off from the parent company and sent to a subsidiary;
- wives of regular employees and those nearing retirement asked to leave by involuntary retirement;
- retrenchment of employees who have been with the company for the shortest period of time.

The Japanese constitution provides the right to work as a fundamental right of citizens and employers must provide 'just cause' for dismissal. The courts have often taken a strict attitude to determining 'just cause'. It is astounding that legal precedent has documented that employers are not permitted to dismiss people simply because they are inefficient or lazy! To give you an indication of how hard the courts are on the employer, the following cases are extraordinary examples of so called 'abusive dismissal':

- a maintenance man sold wheels which belonged to the company;
- an employee watched a tennis match during work hours and slept during the night shift.

In both instances, the court ruled that the employee was unfairly fired!

So, what may firms do to protect their interests? In his book *Labour Pains and the Gaijin Boss*, Thomas Nevins suggests that poor performance be thoroughly documented and those employees solemnly advised of desired improvements. They should simultaneously be placed in a transitional probationary period with a fixed-term, one-year contract. This would avoid any surprise of sudden termination and make it easier, from a legal perspective, for the employer not to renew the contract.

Other suggested tactics to deal with the poor performer include:

- helping them find another job in a subsidiary company, or the general marketplace;
- placing the employee in a lower level job which they may be better able to handle, or be sufficiently dissatisfied to resign;
- making life in the workplace generally difficult for them so they resign voluntarily.

I, personally, would not advocate the latter. It is better

to be direct with the poor performer and indicate that, if they do not improve, it would be necessary to sever the working relationship. Give them a chance to lift their game, document the performance concerns for them to see and set a time frame in which to see measurable improvement. If all else fails, suggest it would be in their best interest to seek alternate employment by a certain date. This would allow them to save face and cause minimal disruption to other workers.

Because work has traditionally been such an integral part of a Japanese employee's identity, it is important for them to preserve some semblance of dignity, if forced to change jobs. It is not uncommon for a fired worker to still go to work each day because he cannot bring himself to tell his family that he has been sacked.

All employers with a staff of more than ten must have work rules. This requires that they give a worker 30 days notice. A worker, in return, must give the employer 14 days notice. However, in practice, this is seldom the case.

Once someone resigns, companies are obliged to make payment for the mandatory time frame. However, depending on the goodwill between the two parties, the employee may well be immediately escorted out the door. This reduces the likelihood of a departing worker negatively influencing others through implication that there may be better places to work.

Resignations may not always be due to dissatisfaction with the employer or a better offer elsewhere. Employees may voluntarily resign if they feel they have disgraced the company in any way. This is particularly true in executive ranks. It is not uncommon for managing directors to offer their resignation if some serious infringement of ethics occurs in a subsidiary firm which would reflect badly on the parent company.

Refer also to: Discretion . . . and loss of face, Lifelong employment, Obligation, Recruiting, Retirement, Unions, Work ethic

RETIREMENT

Until a few years ago, most workers retired at 55 years of age but 60 has become more the norm in recent times. Government officials are now trying to persuade corporations to further raise the retirement age from 60 to 65. They warn of a 2.6 million shortage of workers in 10 years time if companies don't comply.

To assist firms with a supply of skilled labour, the government has set up 425 employment centres for retired workers, whom they dispatch to companies which request particular talents.

A worker may retire to work for another company. This usually, but not exclusively, occurs in management positions and is often mutually agreed between the companies.

The most common arrangement is for a senior manager, who has reached a plateau in his company, to retire and be re-employed by a subsidiary or supplier.

A few American companies have copied a widespread Japanese practice, by recruiting a senior bureaucrat who retires from the government. This form of hiring people 'in the know' is sometimes referred to as 'a descent from heaven'. Proportionately, Japan has the lowest percentage of the labour force employed in government of any other modern country (see *Kaisha* by Abegglen and Stalk). And senior officials are highly respected for their knowledge.

Many retirees from major firms are still supplied with business cards long after they formally leave the organisation.

Refer also to: Lifelong employment, Seniority

S

SAFETY AND SECURITY

I accidentally left my briefcase in my bicycle basket on a busy street corner. The briefcase itself was worth a few hundred dollars and contained cash over US$2000. I was relieved to rush out of the restaurant ten minutes later and find it sitting just as I had left it!

That is not to say that everyone in Japan is honest but most decent people assume others will be. I once had my scooter stolen. On that occasion, I was not feeling very positive about Japanese honesty and honour. Until . . . I called the dealer from whom I'd purchased the original scooter to enquire about buying another. He was very concerned that 'such a terrible thing would happen'. Rather than sell me another scooter, which I was quite prepared to buy there and then, he offered to lend me, at no charge, another second-hand scooter for a few weeks in case my original scooter showed up. He delivered it to my home and made all the necessary licence plate arrangements at no extra charge. After about six weeks, there was no sign of my original scooter, so I bought the second-hand one from him, most appreciative of the loan.

A few weeks later, the original scooter was found. By this stage, I'd thrown out the keys etc. I called Ishi-*san* and explained what had happened. 'No trouble,' he said. 'Which scooter would you prefer?' He made up keys for the old one, registered and insured both of them on my behalf while I arranged to sell one to a colleague. What do you think that sort of service does for customer loyalty? I must have recommended at least a dozen other people to his shop! We were both pleased with the result.

Security is always a factor for anyone to consider. Even though Tokyo is statistically the safest city in the world per capita, one must still remember that 'per capita' refers to over 20 million inhabitants and it is a danger for any Westerner to automatically assume that it is a totally safe environment. It is foolish to throw caution to the wind because of a false belief that everyone walking the streets is safe.

On my third day in Japan, I was suddenly assaulted by a man who was yelling and hitting me with an umbrella. This was in the middle of the afternoon at a major railway station. I was totally stunned. It was the last thing I expected in the country with the lowest crime rate (per capita!) in the world. It turned out that he was a crazy war veteran who took a sudden dislike to me for no apparent reason, as was explained by an apologetic passerby who came to my rescue.

The Japanese tend to be very thorough in everything they do. I was amazed that we would not only have one, but sometimes two, fire drills in a day. This was to ensure everyone thoroughly understood the procedure. Most companies would have an earthquake disaster plan which would also be rehearsed.

We had instances of an expat teenager being molested in a dark street and numerous house break-ins. I would encourage everyone to take out a household contents insurance policy. A number of IBM employees did not do so because they were under the illusion that Japan was 100 per cent safe. They then expected the company to bear the cost of their loss and were disappointed that we did not. So, never assume that Japan is 'safe'. It's certainly a lot safer than comparably sized cities like New York or London but there are good and bad in every country.

If involved in a traffic accident, remain at the scene and assist if possible. Wait for the police. If you were responsible for injury to an individual, you would be expected to visit with appropriate gifts of flowers or food.

IBM was very security-conscious because of the ready identification with the United States. ID badges were required to enter and leave the premises, which was the norm for most large multinational companies operating in Tokyo. Security measures are usually tightened if there are any major international political conferences or dignitaries in town.

Occasionally, you will see right-wing activists driving up main streets in trucks and shouting abuse through loud megaphones. These are usually in protest against Russian occupation of the northernmost Japanese islands but these handful of demonstrators have a general dislike of foreigners. Their presence can be a bit disconcerting at first but the police carefully monitor their activity and there is nothing to fear.

The key rule is to be neither complacent nor paranoid.

Refer also to: Earthquakes, Medical, Obligation, Typhoons

SALARY

The subject of salaries is a complex one indeed. It is not the intent of this chapter to explore the vast array of remuneration packages or specific monetary values, which are constantly changing, but simply to outline a few principles which are generally applicable.

Salaries are almost always linked to the bonus system. Individuals receive a significant portion of their pay in their annual or semi-annual bonus, which is directly linked to the performance of the company.

Like Western companies, there is no single formula for calculating an individual's worth to an organisation, and a great deal of subjectivity is involved. Unlike Western companies, employees performing the same task with the same degree of competence do not necessarily receive the same pay. Men and older employees still obtain higher salaries for doing the same job. Recent steps forward in equal opportunity legislation may alter this inequity.

Annual increases are calculated based on only approximately 60 per cent merit. The remaining 40 per cent depends on length of service and age (which are usually related).

Salary scales are such that it is most unlikely that a high school graduate would ever exceed the salary level of a university graduate, regardless of long-term performance.

Deductions for the national pension fund are compulsory for all workers, regardless of nationality.

However, it seems unfair that foreigners, who are forced to contribute to this scheme, are not eligible to benefit from it upon retirement.

Although income distribution in Japan is far from equal, the gulf in remuneration between workers and executives is far less than other developed countries. Japanese executives generally receive substantially lower salaries than their American, Australian or British counterparts. Even if extensive fringe benefits such as housing are taken into account, the Japanese executive's remuneration package does not match that of his Western competitors. In today's business environment, these large differences can certainly not be explained on the basis of profitability; unless the relationship is inverse!

Compared to the executive, the average worker is remunerated rather well compared to workers in other advanced countries. However, one must carefully examine precisely what is meant by 'average wage'. This usually includes overtime and the typical worker in Japan would generally put in a lot of overtime; much of it at overtime rates.

Overtime payments are common for most employees, except those who reach middle to senior management ranks. This is but one explanation as to why workers are at the office so late. The overtime supplement to the salary is often a factor counted on when balancing the household budget. I would be reluctant to state the case, but it is at least conceivable, that work may be stretched out over a longer time frame than necessary if the employee is eligible for overtime payments.

In addition to a basic salary, overtime payments and

bonuses, the Japanese worker is usually provided with a number of fringe benefits by the company. These range from subsidised accommodation to low-cost memberships in sports clubs. Managers and executives spend a great deal of money on entertainment, which is always considered a company expense.

Foreigners who are full-time contracted employees of Japanese or foreign firms have compulsory pension deductions of approximately 10–12 per cent taken from their monthly salary. Costs are often shared by the employee and employer on a 50:50 basis but many overseas firms will underwrite the entire amount since foreign workers are *not* reimbursed for payments made to the plan unless they have lived in Japan for more than 20 years.

Refer also to: Allowances and benefits, Bonus, Entertainment, Work ethic

SENIORITY

Don't be at all surprised if a recent acquaintance eagerly asks your age within the early stages of conversation. Unlike Western society, this is not regarded as rude and there is no pretence of coyness. Many Japanese are curious to know one's age because seniority still brings a degree of respect. And, in many work situations, a person will attempt to estimate your position in the hierarchy by virtue of age. This is a far from accurate means of determining status but usually provides a rough approximation if dealing with a traditional Japanese firm. It is difficult to gauge the age of Japanese and it is not considered rude to ask.

Even if a senior person is actually lower in the management hierarchy, there is an unwritten rule of conduct that more junior employees should still treat them with respect and seek their assistance to complete tasks.

Seniority in a company is still generally highly regarded, even though the more senior person may not necessarily be the leader or decision maker. When doing business with Japanese firms these days, it is important to cultivate not only the 'senior' executives but the middle managers.

The older you are, the more pay you will receive for doing the same job. Professor Haruo Shimada, professor of economics at Keio University, presented the following figures to an industrial relations seminar at Massachusetts Institute of Technology in 1982: 'Japanese age/wage profiles share considerable similarity with profiles for American workers except for the pattern of age differentials for the younger age range (who earn considerably less).'

The ageing work force in Japan will result in higher salary budgets for companies and ultimately reduce global competitiveness if all other factors remain the same.

Be sensitive to the still-ingrained respect for seniority but do not overlook talented younger employees for recognition because of this. It may not always be desirable to promote them to a management role but it is important to give them ample recognition for their contribution, especially in cases where they may be 'carrying' an older employee. Recognition may be subtle, possibly in the form of a business trip or training program overseas, and a few private words which indicate you feel they are worthwhile. It used to be thought that promoting a 'young Turk' would deter them from ultimate success. One should certainly be cautious and not move with undue haste but youth, alone, is no excuse to hold them back.

Many young people are becoming increasingly frustrated by the traditional system of seniority. As firms see they are in danger of losing some of their brightest talent to more Westernised organisations, the system of seniority is slowly becoming less important—but I suspect it will take some time to see any visible change.

Promotions of any sort traditionally occur in April and October.

Those who make it to the top of Japanese companies are usually those with the best interpersonal skills. They are equally skilled at human resource management as they are at decision making or specific functional tasks. They set the tone and correct environment for others to make the right decisions and develop the necessary skills and strategies for a successful organisation.

Akio Morita, the Chairman of Sony, writes: 'In Japan, the most successful leader in business is not the man who goes around giving detailed instructions to his subordinates. It is the man who gives his subordinates only general guidelines and instils confidence in them and helps them to do good work' (Morita, A. *Made in Japan*, Collins). This is testimony that the leader may not necessarily have the most foresight or drive but be the best talented to harness the collective resources of the enterprise.

Refer also to: Bowing, Discretion . . . and loss of face, Lifelong employment, Obligation, Resignation and retrenchment, Salary, Work ethic

SERVICE

There is an old adage: 'The only time you get waited on hand and foot is when you get charged an arm and a leg'. Anyone who has visited Japan will testify that nothing is cheap. Interestingly enough, US-based research shows that customers are willing to pay more for the same product *if* they get better service.

Service is intangible. It's not a definable product with a shelf life. It is only as good as what is being delivered at that point in time, by that particular person. Good service is not given by organisations but by individuals within those organisations. That is why it is critical that the human resource factor should not be overlooked. It is far more than a cliché to simply say that people are the most valuable asset. And, how management treats those people will be noticed by customers directly or indirectly.

There are many publications devoted entirely to this subject. I have written one myself, and it would be inappropriate to propose theories and strategies for superior service within the context of this particular text. I wish to simply provide a broad overview of the benefits of superior service and illustrate a few real-life examples of quality service in Japan. These examples, from a wide variety of businesses, are testimony to the Japanese notion that providing good service is, in fact, an honourable deed in all facets of endeavour.

In Western society, we tend to think of service jobs as

those which you do when you don't have adequate skills to get another (such as working your way through university by serving hamburgers, or washing cars, or baby sitting). We often regard service jobs as means to ends, rather than a fulfilling and valuable endeavour in themselves. The first thing which needs to be remembered is that service is *not* subservience, which our Western materialistic mentality too often suggests. In fact, there are two dictionary definitions of service: the attendance of an inferior upon a superior; and to be useful.

To remain competitive, we must instil in both our executives and frontline employees that the second definition is the preferred one; and there should be no inference that serving is beneath anyone's dignity. It is to be useful and excellent service should be encouraged and rewarded by management.

As service increasingly becomes a differentiating feature and competitive edge in the marketplace, human resource strategies must focus on ensuring the organisation and the people within it are prepared to deliver nothing short of superior service.

Here are a few examples of everyday service in Japan, examples which, I believe, demonstrate the service mentality which permeates all walks of life.

When I first moved into my apartment, I was accompanied by the realtor plus two blue-suited maintenance men. Between the three of them, they carefully showed me how to use all the appliances in the place. I must say that a PhD in electronics still wouldn't have adequately prepared me to handle my fully-programmable air-conditioning unit and the oven that played Lithuanian folk songs when cooking time had expired! But I was less impressed by this array of marvellous technology than I was by the fantastic service they were providing, and their concern that I should be happy to live in the building. The realtor also introduced me to the caretaker and explained that if I wanted any laundry done, I could leave it with him to arrange pickup and delivery. As a working woman, I thought I'd died and gone to heaven. What a wonderful welcome to Japan.

I was astounded and delighted that this was not an isolated example of the service mentality in Japan.

I'm not sure who I was expecting to call me in Tokyo but I felt a need to own an answering machine. I purchased this device from a delightful young Japanese man who had studied law in New Zealand. He not only installed it but also showed me how to use it (because all the instructions were in Japanese and German). He phoned a few days later to see if I was happy with it. As it turned out, I was more than happy with the machine but had received rather few calls as I had been at home with a terrible flu. Much to my surprise, he arrived at the door a couple of hours later with roses, chocolates, corn flakes, milk and fruit!

Let's look at a more traditional service sector; one which could be seen, by those who don't know any better, as a subservient task. For most of my career, I have hired cleaners because it's a chore I never particularly enjoyed or seemed to find time to do. At first, I found a need to rationalise the expense by surmising that the people I hired were better skilled than me (which is true) and I was helping the economy by providing employment. You see, I had bought into the stigma that women (whether working or not) should still attend to domestic duties. The cleaners would vacuum, dust, wash floors etc. Naturally, I would dutifully tidy up the night before they arrived and do a bit of the more detailed work after they left.

That was before I met the wonderful Ishizaka-*san*. She was an elderly woman who looked too tiny and frail to control even a medium sized vacuum. In fact, she was literally shorter than a broomstick. But, if there was a Hall of Fame for Cleaners, she would most certainly be a star. Not only did she do the basic vacuuming, dusting, floors, toilets and sinks, but she polished all brass and silver, procured and watered plants, did the washing and ironing and mended clothes. I thought all my Christmases had come at once and was more than happy with the outstanding service she provided, with no direction from me.

But Ishizaka-*san*, had a major problem. One day she phoned my secretary and complained, 'DeVrye-*san* is too clean and tidy. I do not have enough work to do during a day. Please tell her that I will also cook meals for her on Wednesdays and make sure she is home before I leave at 5.00 p.m. so the food does not get cold.'

I was astounded. This woman took such pride in her work, was so willing to be of service and wanted to be viewed favourably. It actually took a great deal of convincing for her to realise that the chances of my getting home from work by 5.00 p.m. were as remote as me polishing my own silver. We eventually compromised that she would wash the outside balcony whether it needed it or not and do some shopping. Can you imagine a cleaner in Australia or the United States, to whom you pay a flat rate, regardless of hours worked, doing all that and then asking for more?

Management and shop-floor employees alike embrace the notion of providing superior service to customers. Any form of deliberate inconvenience to a customer is regarded as sabotage, rather than simply a slowdown. Most workers who go on strike recognise the importance of the customer to their own hip pocket.

If workers go on strike and plan to cut a public service in any way, they must notify the public well in advance so there is minimum disruption. That is the stated law although on one occasion in three years (yes, only one), the trains went on strike and regardless of any notification, this was still a huge inconvenience to the millions of commuters.

The previous example was one of the few isolated cases of bad service that I can recall in Japan. Most times, service was exemplary and it is far easier to recall positive experiences.

Although I enjoyed my stay in Japan, I was pleased to return home to Australia. What I didn't find pleasing was the comparatively poor service levels, when I had come to expect good service as a way of life.

I guess that I should have stopped being astounded at the extraordinary service I received in Japan, but it simply never ceased to amaze me. Everyone I spoke to had similar tales of service excellence, whether it be in a business environment or on the street, where people will literally go miles out of their way to help a stranded tourist.

It's not just a matter of believing that superior service, like motherhood, is a good thing. It's a matter of instilling a notion throughout a nation that it is not beneath anyone's dignity to provide excellent service; that it is an admirable and honourable thing to do.

You may cynically say that few Westerners would have the opportunity to live in Japan and experience superior service first hand. One could argue that if customers haven't had that experience of great service, the average person will be happy with mediocre service. But just ask General Motors or Ford what Toyota and Honda are doing to raise customer expectations (and market share!) in the United States and Australia.

The feeling of pride in providing superior service is what gives the Japanese a competitive advantage as they expand into international markets. They are raising the service bar for everyone. Others need to do likewise; not to copy the Japanese but to strive to exceed their own unique brand of customer expectations.

I'm not sure if the Japanese deliver better service because they are not constantly driven by having to return quarterly results to shareholders and can, therefore, take a more long-term view. That is one excuse given by Westerners as to why they can't offer similar service excellence. However, this doesn't adequately explain why bus drivers bow when their passengers alight; why staff at food stops do likewise when passengers depart; and why garbage men take pride in having sparkling clean trucks. There were even 24-hour garbage bin deposits in my apartment complex.

The challenge for the Japanese is to maintain their high

levels of service as more and more young people in their culture are becoming increasingly Westernised and picking up both the best and worst of that inter-nationalism.

We need to get away from the notion in the West that frontline staff are only doing those jobs until such time or because they are unable to obtain a management job. The forward-thinking managers of the 1990s must create a positive climate towards customer service in their organisation. This is, admittedly, harder to do in countries which do not have the traditional Japanese approach as a nation to service; and the employee group is less homogeneous. Difficult, it may be. Optional, it is not!

Refer also to: Food, Postal, Quality, Shopping, Transport, Unions, Work ethic

SHOPPING

In Tokyo, Western supermarkets are available with most things you can buy at home. It was reassuring to see familiar brand names but not quite as comforting to notice the price tags. Goods are more expensive in suburbs close to the central business district where many Westerners choose to live. It's much cheaper to shop at small, local Japanese shops which are not in the heart of the city. Expect to pay substantially more for any item in neighbourhoods such as Ginza, Roppongi and Hiroo (the latter is referred to as Gaijin Ghetto because it is so popular with foreigners). After a few weeks, I learned where bargains could be obtained but still usually chose to shop in Hiroo, simply because the shops located under my apartment complex were so convenient.

Clothing and especially shoes are often difficult to find in large sizes. I recall with horror my first shopping excursion to a department store. I was carefully guided toward the maternity ward as the tiny saleslady was quite sure anyone of my 173 cm frame wouldn't fit into normal sizes! So it is important to bring a supply of sturdy footwear as you will be doing a lot of walking.

Other things to bring from home include:

• Bedding, if you are bringing your own bed,
because sizes of Japanese beds and linen are different.
• Medication.
• Favourite chocolate or treats.

I know of some assignees who shipped over mass quantities of toilet paper, cartons of canned produce and stockpiled other non-perishable goods, which were available in Japan but more expensive. If shipment provisions allow, it's not a bad idea to bring some extra supplies of consumable goods until such time as you have a better idea of where to go to shop. I had some spare room in my shipment so brought extra shampoo, hygiene products, peanut butter etc. but soon discovered I could obtain it all locally.

I was delighted that retail shops were open until 10.00 p.m. and also on Saturdays and Sundays—a big bonus, especially for a working woman. I could even have my hair cut any day of the week, with a neck and upper back massage thrown in for free. Many department stores and local shops were closed one day per week. This varied from store to store but if one was closed, another was generally open.

On aspects of home delivery . . . my morning newspaper always managed to be delivered to the door and not the bushes. More astoundingly, the supermarket would deliver groceries within thirty minutes of when they said they would, for no extra charge if you bought more than a certain amount. If you bought frozen products, the checkout person would always ask 'How many minutes?'—meaning how far your home is from the supermarket so they could estimate how much dry ice to pack with the frozen goods to keep them from melting.

One or two major Tokyo supermarkets provide catalogues (in English, French and German) whereby you can order goods over the phone and have them delivered to your door.

The supermarket arrangement in Japan was such that you ordered soft drinks at the checkout rather than collect them and put them in your trolley. One day, I arrived home to a message on my answering machine, saying they forgot to charge me for the soft drink. However, by the time I received the message, the delivery boy had already been and I was simply asked to pay for the goods next time I happened to be in the shop!

What do you think that sort of service does to generate customer loyalty? They look at the customer–trader relationship as a partnership based on mutual trust.

Top sales personnel in stores really know their regular customers. They make it their business to learn their likes and dislikes, lifestyles and tastes. When they deliver goods to the home, they may casually observe the interior decor and make suggestions. They keep a list of customers' birthdays, gifts bought for family members in the past, and offer suggestions for the future.

Customers are also tangibly rewarded for repeat business. My local hairdresser, bakery, vegetable shop and service station all gave me a card, not unlike a credit card. Every time I used their goods or services, I received a stamp. After a set amount of visits, I received some free merchandise. It certainly encouraged me to return. The local bakery even gave out free bread to regular customers on their first anniversary.

Refer also to: Food, Gift giving, Service

SMOKING

As you gasp your way through most offices, it may be hard to believe smoking is starting to become an employee relations issue. Like progressive Western companies, management of major firms are looking at ways to address this problem; but Japan has certainly not moved into the age of the smoke-free workplace.

A research group of the Tobacco Problems Information Centre recently surveyed 460 companies and 123 local governments. Only 135 organisations responded, which represents less than a quarter of the sample. Of those who replied, 61 per cent indicated they were taking 'some' action to deal with smoking in the workplace. It would probably be safe to assume that the 75 per cent who did not respond have no intention of addressing the issue.

Very few firms have banned smoking, but certain enlightened ones (excuse my obvious bias) are at least starting to: restrict smoking hours; set aside non-smoking areas; or offer programs to help employees quit smoking.

Refer also to: Hygiene factors

Sport and Recreation

Most businesses have active social clubs which receive encouragement and partial sponsorship from management. They organise outings to such events as baseball games, movies, ski resorts and Disneyland.

The majority of large firms now take recreation as a serious component of employee benefits. At Canon, for instance, there are 36 athletic clubs, which have 25 tennis courts, 5 gymnasiums, 17 cultural clubs, swimming pools etc. I spent the occasional afternoon at the IBM complex, which had tennis courts, baseball, gridiron, rugby and table tennis available.

Because of the scarcity of space, even these company facilities need to be booked well in advance. The demand is often so great that bookings are done on a lottery basis, which is usually administered by the personnel department. Employees interested in obtaining a booking state their preferred time by a certain date. If more than one party requests that time, names are put into a hat and the lucky winner is selected at random.

Company holiday homes in the mountains or at the beach may also be allocated on a lottery basis. Some companies keep these venues for the exclusive use of executives but many make them available to employees on a free or heavily subsidised basis.

There were *ikebana* (flower-arranging) classes in our

cafeteria after work but I must confess to being an *ikebana* dropout. My typical Western impatience just wouldn't let my mind understand why it took 20–30 minutes to decide how to place one flower in an arrangement! But, then again, there was a lot which my mind never fully comprehended.

And some of that lack of comprehension didn't relate to the Japanese side of recreation. I'm still not at all sure that IBM made the best business decision by providing all expatriate employees with automatic membership to the Tokyo American Club. There is absolutely nothing wrong with this excellent facility and it serves a useful purpose in the community. However, membership is expensive and I would question why any organisation would automatically pay for expatriates to become members, when many would in no way take full advantage of such a membership, nor appreciate the considerable cost which the company had underwritten. There are also limits to the number of members any club can comfortably accommodate and at times the waiting list may preclude joining for months or even years.

However, it is important for any visitors to a strange country to have outlets for stress and recreation and any expatriate package in Japan should make a generous allowance for recreational activities, which are much more expensive than in any other country. There are various debates as to whether this should be rolled into the overall compensation package or designated as a special allocation which may be used only for recreational pursuits.

One argument would say that it is no business of the company to determine what is a 'suitable' recreation activity. Nevertheless, I would recommend that a separate allowance be denoted to provide tangible encouragement for employees to make an effort to engage in activities other than work to help reduce the inevitable stress which accompanies them on assignment. Such an allowance may take the form of a cash allowance or percentage of membership paid in a club. A 'user pays' component is also desirable because the research is quite conclusive that if people receive something for nothing, that is exactly what they tend to think it is worth. Whereas, if they make a personal financial contribution, their commitment to pursuing a healthy recreation is more likely; which may even contribute to increased productivity on the job.

Although recreational activities are certainly not as readily accessible as most Westerners would be used to, there is an increasing variety of leisure time pursuits which can be pursued with 'relative' ease. One must, by necessity, use the word 'relative' in relation to recreation in Tokyo. You may be fortunate enough to live near a neighbourhood aerobics centre or have a swimming pool in your apartment complex, but the majority of expatriates must seek out such opportunities.

It is possible to purchase summer memberships in many major hotel swimming pools, a welcome relief from the Tokyo humidity. There has been a recent upsurge in local aerobics classes, squash courts and multitiered golf driving ranges, because they all make reasonably effective use of precious space. The challenge for the non-Japanese-speaking foreigner is to discover the details of where these are located without becoming more stressed out in the process of trying to eliminate stress!

I employed a university student for a summer job to compile a 'Fun and fitness' guide to Tokyo which we distributed to our assignees. It contained over 40 pages of reference material on where to locate recreational facilities, costs involved etc.

Virtually every type of activity is available if one is willing to invest what is usually more travelling time than you would be used to in your home country. Activities include aerobics, archery, badminton, basketball, bicycling, bowling, camping, country clubs, darts, equestrian, excursions, fishing, golf, ice hockey, ice skating, martial arts, orienteering, parks and gardens, racquetball, resorts, roller skating, rowing, skiing, softball, sports clubs, squash, swimming pools, tennis, volleyball.

Families could also spend a day walking around a giant maze. I found this rather unnecessary as I seemed continually lost in everyday streets, without the need to visit any amusement park.

In years to come, it may be that some of the seven million skiers in the country do not venture onto a 'real' mountain to ski. The world's largest indoor ski field is scheduled for completion in 1995. A 234-metre-high cone, 700 metres in diameter, will sport six slopes that 7000 people from beginners to experts can use at one time. Visitors may park 15 000 cars inside the vast dome, shop at a department store and stay in a 1700-room hotel.

Sumo is a very popular spectator sport. During key matches, which finish around 5.30 p.m., it would not be uncommon to see employees leave the office to watch the event on a nearby television. Domestic flights are sometimes delayed because passengers refuse to board the aircraft during the dying moments of a crucial match.

Sumo ranks with golf as the most favoured way to entertain key clients in Japan. Corporate boxes are very exclusive, with an elaborate array of food and drink served to those customers valued enough to be invited. The price of obtaining such corporate boxes may be equivalent to hundreds of thousands of US dollars.

According to *The Sydney Morning Herald* of 9 January 1991, there is now robot sumo whereby different robots are pitted against each other to go through the motions of the sumo wrestler. The implication to management in Japan is somewhat remote but one engineer was quoted as saying: 'I can't think of a single useful thing I could do with this robot' as he looked upon his robot which had just been defeated in competition. Then he brightened up and added, 'Maybe I could teach it to attack my boss!'.

The Japanese love their sport. Skiing, tennis and aerobics are cited as the most popular. However, Japanese participants have expectations quite different from those of Westerners. I once met a young woman on a chair lift and we struck up a conversation about skiing. She mentioned that she had skied in the Rocky Mountains where I had grown up. I thought we would develop instant rapport when I commented on the short lift lines, long runs and uncrowded conditions by comparison to the south island of Japan where there seemed to be ten people for every snowflake. I was astounded when she firmly informed me that she much preferred Japanese conditions because the reduced crowds and longer runs in Lake Louise meant you had to ski longer so there was less time for recovery, making it a very tiring sport!

There are two lessons here. First, never assume that everyone adheres to Western standards of 'goodness' in either a recreational or a business setting. Second, make sure you alter your expectations of ideal recreation standards while resident in Japan.

I once journeyed many hours to Tsutsumigawa Beach, which was proudly advertised on a tourist brochure as one of the best beaches in Japan. Upon further investigation, when I was sure I had arrived at the wrong location, I learned I was in fact at the proper destination. This was, contrary to my doubt, the famous shore which had 300 *metres* of unspoiled beach. I admittedly was expecting something more akin to Ninety *Mile* Beach on Australia's southern coast. Never again will I take for granted the spaciousness of Canada or Australia. But it was a hot, sunny day so I had little choice (apart from being grumpy) but to alter my expectations and enjoy it for what it was.

If one is feeling stressed after a hectic day in Tokyo, you can dial a masseur to visit your home. Now, before imaginations run wild, let me emphasise that this is a totally legitimate shiatsu massage of major muscle groups only! What a great way to relax.

Refer also to: Baseball, Entertainment, Golf, Lotteries

T

TAX

Foreign residents have a responsibility to meet their tax obligation in Japan, as well as their home country. Because of the complexities involved, the key is simply to obtain the services of a reputable tax accountant who is familiar with both countries' legislation. Your consulate should be able to provide a list of such qualified accountants.

Refer also to : Legal matters

TEAMWORK

The Frank Sinatra song 'My Way' is surprisingly popular in Japan, in a society which more readily refers to 'We' than 'I'.

Teamwork is central to the Japanese work ethos and is evident from formal decision making to casual entertainment. It is probably best known for the success of quality circles in the workplace. There can be no doubt that cohesive teamwork pays dividends. Again, there are a plethora of books which outline means to achieve this unity of purpose.

I must confess to only partially embracing the concept due to my firmly entrenched belief that individual effort deserves reward. I had read that management should not single out any one person for recognition in a group because it would embarrass them. I chose to ignore this advice and believed it was yet another of the many sweeping statements we had come to believe about the Japanese workplace.

I was wrong in one particular instance. On this occasion, I decided, against all advice, to give a substantial cheque and framed certificate to one employee for his outstanding contribution. He had devised a system which saved our business hundreds of thousands of dollars. He was a young man, who had studied overseas. I assumed he would be appreciative of this recognition and financial reward. You can imagine my surprise when, in his acceptance speech, he apologised to co-workers for being singled out and then praised them, stating how much more worthy they were. He spent the entire sum (and possibly more) treating them all to dinner.

I was ready to admit defeat and concur that this was an instance where the textbooks were entirely correct in their guidance. That is, until a colleague told me of a similar situation where the individual concerned simply said thank you and gratefully pocketed the cheque to purchase some consumer item.

So once again, I can only state that there can be no single rule for dealing with situations. I know it must be getting repetitive and boring for the reader to consistently read 'no generalisations' but . . . no generalisations!

Refer also to: Communication . . . and useful phrases, Decisions, Discretion . . . and loss of face, Entertainment, Lunches, Lifelong employment, Meetings, Parties, Quality

TELEPHONES

The installation of a telephone is very expensive if the residence does not already have one installed. However, many homes now have the wiring in place and it is a simple matter for the telephone company to connect the new line. I was most impressed at the ability to make firm arrangements for the date and time of the telephone workers to arrive.

Like long distance calls, even local calls are timed and charged for every three minutes.

Public phones are readily available and take coins or phone cards. Phone cards display popular graphics and become collectors' items, following their practical use.

Refer also to: Communication . . . and useful phrases

TEMPORARIES

Temporaries are the lowest form of life in a Japanese company. The organisation has no paternal sense of obligation to provide them with lifetime employment and the associated benefits. They are used extensively to balance human resources by enabling extra staff to be employed in good times with no qualms about retrenchment in bad. When times are tough, temporaries are simply asked to terminate employment. It is a practice referred to as *katatataki*, which stands for a 'tap on the shoulder'. It is almost that simple. The company can do this with ease because there was never any implied commitment to temporary staff by offering the status of full-time employment.

Part-time workers receive a pay packet approximately three-quarters that of full-timers doing the identical job. Only about 10 per cent of companies offer them any health or retirement benefits, or severance pay. Temporaries are placed on contracts at the time of employment, even though they may do exactly the same thing as full-time employees.

It is estimated that the 4.2 million part-time workers comprise nearly 10 per cent of Japan's labour force; most of whom are in smaller firms. Naturally, it comes as no surprise that over 90 per cent are women.

Part-time employees are not organised into unions so their lot is unlikely to improve.

Refer also to: Lifelong employment, Unions, Work ethic

TOILETS

Always carry tissues with you in Japan because public toilets, even in some of the better-known department stores, do not always stock such a basic commodity. No one has been able to explain this to my satisfaction but there is some speculation that it relates to the countrywide toilet paper shortage in the early 1980's. As a result, owners of public places felt it was risking too much loss of face if they ran out, so they abolished it completely.

Many toilets do not have seats and you need to simply squat over a hole. One theory claims that Japanese are not as competitive in international sport because they are increasingly using Western toilets so their thigh muscles are less developed, because they assume the sitting versus the squatting position!

At the other extreme, I never ceased to be amazed when I encountered a heated toilet seat. Admittedly, this was particularly pleasant in winter months but I remained unimpressed by the blow dryers attached to some; apparently a Japanese innovation following the toilet paper shortage!

Refer also to: Transport

TRADITION

Tradition is very important in Japan. However, in the age of internationalism, no company operating in Japan can afford to be bamboozled by sticking to tradition (Japanese or otherwise), unless those traditions are assessed to be appropriate for today's competitive environment.

It is wise for a foreigner operating in Japan to be sensitive to the traditions of the country but foolish not to evaluate those traditions in relation to the issue at hand. Nothing is more frustrating than to ask the question 'Why?' only to be informed: 'Because it is the Japanese way'.

For the Japanese worker with a foreign boss, this has proved to be an easy answer to forestall change. Many a foreigner feels intimidated by this reply and is reluctant to probe further. Don't hesitate to pursue: '*Why* is it the Japanese way?'.

Research shows that most employees, worldwide, are hesitant to change. Don't accept standard replies if you are to remain competitive. Enquire further: 'Is this *Japanese way*, which was once very successful, appropriate today?'. If so, ask for justification as to *why* it is still considered valid.

One tradition that *is* worth following is that of not losing your temper in public or publicly criticising an employee. If you do display anger, it will not only damage relationships with that person (which may be of no consequence to you if you are unhappy with their performance), you will also lose respect from others, who will see you as a person who cannot control emotions.

Refer also to: Every other entry

Transfers

It is common practice for Japanese companies with national and international branches to transfer employees to those locations. This is no different from Western practice except staff are often sent for periods of up to 2–3 years without their families!

It is estimated that nearly 200 000 workers currently fall into this category each year. The practice is referred to as *Tanshin funin* and, surprisingly, has not yet become a union issue.

This is amazing, in that two government surveys provided evidence that the practice is not popular amongst the work force, 48 per cent of employees stating that they strongly opposed transfer without their families. Another 42 per cent indicated they would be willing to move only if there were compelling reasons to do so.

The results of these surveys were published in the 6 December 1987 edition of *Japan Times*, which also ran an editorial comment on the findings: 'With all the pressures for increasing individual freedom seen in contemporary society, we can expect an increase in the attitude that questions why the company's convenience should take precedence over the family's'.

It is important that this survey, like all statistics, be put in perspective. While many families may not relish the prospect of being transferred to an industrial location in Japan, the results would be quite different if a destination such as Paris was specified.

The question of transferring dual-career families is seldom a major consideration in Japan these days but may well become one as the move towards Western norms increases and more women assume professional duties.

Refer also to: Lifelong employment, Obligation, Resignation and retrenchment, Retirement

TRANSPORT

Over 2500 trains pass through Tokyo Central Station each day and everyone in my suburb seemed determined to board the same carriage as me every morning. During peak times, there are 'shovers' employed by the railways to compress as many people as possible into a carriage. These men wear immaculate white gloves and as their title suggests, gently shove people into the car before the door closes. Being taller than the average Japanese, I always arrived at the office feeling someone was still nestled comfortably in my armpit. Do not be offended if you are jostled in what Westerners would regard as rude shoving and undue close proximity.

The only saving grace was that the trains provided a service I haven't experienced in Australia and the United States. They ran on time. They were clean and adequately staffed so that they were safe to ride at all hours.

Women are occasionally groped. It is nearly impossible to identify the offender in the crowd so the best tactic is to ignore.

A worker is not necessarily a pervert if he's seen ogling a pornographic comic book in full view on the subway—a lot of others do likewise.

Never sit on the silver seat of a train as these are reserved for the elderly. Even if no one publicly admonished you, it would be an embarrassment.

Rush hours are chaos and to be avoided if you are

travelling with any luggage or small children. Many signs in the Tokyo area are now in English and people are very helpful. You can purchase special discounts for weekly or monthly fares on suburban trains and the famous inter-city 'bullet trains' are a delight to travel on.

Buses are another popular means of transport but the routes are not as easy to comprehend as the train system, and less information is available in English. However, once you learnt a certain method of reaching a destination, this could be a useful alternative to trains.

Monorail is available to some destinations, including Haneda airport. Speaking of airports, it is very expensive to take a taxi from the international airport due to the distance and traffic congestion. Most locals and visitors alike take a bus or train to Tokyo City Air Terminal (T-CAT) and then easily catch a local train or cab from there to their final destination.

Many expatriates claim taxis will not stop for them on the street, especially late at night. There must be some truth that they don't want to hassle with Westerners who don't speak the language or are probably only going to be a short fare (because most Westerners live close to downtown Tokyo), but I have personally never experienced this and my memories of taxis in Japan are nothing but favourable. (Although it did take a while to get used to drivers unceremoniously relieving themselves against telephone poles, but never when the cab had a passenger.) Taxis show up on time. Vehicles are spotlessly clean, usually with white seat covers. The driver wears white gloves and dims his lights at intersections as a courtesy to the driver in the car ahead. Beware that the left-hand door opens automatically as you enter and exit. No tip is expected.

One word of warning . . . residences and streets in Tokyo do not have street numbers and many times a taxi driver has no idea of where to go, especially in residential areas. That is why many people have business cards with a map of the immediate vicinity surrounding their home on the back of the card.

Scooters are very fuel-efficient but the local service station owner always greeted me like I drove a gas guzzler. There was no such thing as self-serve and service stations actually deserved the name. They did, in fact, provide tangible service to customers. Car windscreens were cleaned, ashtrays emptied. Even the mirror on my scooter was regularly wiped.

No customer was too small or trivial not to be treated like an important guest. Often, you were provided with a cool drink as these events took place. The washrooms were incredibly clean and many had freshly cut flowers. I would have much preferred toilet paper.

Refer also to: Automobiles, Toilets

TYPHOONS

The typhoon season usually begins in June and ends in October. It is referred to as the 'rainy season'.

The only good thing about typhoons is that the air is remarkably clear for a few days after one has passed.

Small typhoons are common and there is usually little impact on business. However, as a manager you should be sure staff are aware of the procedure to follow:

- Ensure there is enough food for 3–4 days.
- Bring indoors all items such as garbage cans, lawn furniture, pot plants and anything else which could blow away or cause destruction.
- Refrain from using elevators because electric power may be shut off.
- Check emergency lighting equipment such as candles and torches.
- Keep radios tuned to an English-speaking channel to see if conditions are likely to deteriorate.
- Secure all doors and windows.
- Draw all curtains, blinds and shutters to minimise any effects of shattered glass.
- Avoid unnecessary trips out of doors.

Refer also to: Earthquakes

U

UNIONS

Fewer hours are lost in Japan due to industrial disputes than in any country except West Germany.

According to the *Japan Statistical Yearbook*, there were 1292 labour disputes in 1991, compared to 4826 in 1985. There is no precise definition of what constitutes a 'dispute' but the trend appears to be towards fewer disputes, however defined, since 1984, when Japan lost 354 000 man days. This is an exceptionally low figure compared to the United States, which lost 8 348 000, and the United Kingdom, which sacrificed a staggering 26 564 000 days as a result of union unrest.

Why do the Japanese lose 75 times fewer work days than their British counterparts? What is so unique about industrial relations in Japan that construction workers on a building site would actually buy a New Year's wreath out of their own pocket, as a symbol to wish the company prosperity in the year ahead?

One answer lies in the notion of enterprise unions, which are predominant in Japan. These represent all members of the same company, regardless of skill. Due to the close relationship with one firm, the union obviously has a vested interest to see that particular organisation prosper.

According to Professor Haruo Shimada of Keio University, more than 90 per cent of Japanese unions are organised on the basis of the enterprise; and more than 80 per cent of unionised workers are represented by such enterprise unions.

The main function of enterprise unions is collective bargaining. But it is collective bargaining with a difference. The benefits received by workers are closely linked to the profitability of the company. Therefore, it is clearly in the interest of the rank and file to support management, rather than act as an Achilles heel.

There is extensive joint consultation between management and union representatives. Meetings are held regularly, and at least once per month. There is an interchange of information on various matters relating to management policies, production plans, working conditions, fringe benefits etc. Management not only relays decisions to keep workers informed, but also allows the opportunity for open discussion of current concerns.

The unions' legally protected rights include the right of representation on management committees. Any disciplinary punishment must be provided in the work rules or collective agreement. If a firm is unionised, the collective agreement takes precedence over the work rules.

Cooperation is such that the employer may provide the union with office space, contributions to the union welfare fund and other gestures of assistance which would be regarded as most unusual in the West.

In tough times, management first introduces reductions in executive salaries before approaching the union for a cut in employee wages. This is known as the 'Spring Offensive' because it occurs around springtime (April). Most negotiations for improved compensation commence at this time, so it is the season in which strikes are most prevalent.

Many of these are of a non-crippling nature. Employees may go on strike before work or at lunch hour! You can only actually determine that staff are on strike because they wear a black armband and hand out leaflets outlining their case. They smile and are polite to passers-by. It seems there is seldom anything offensive about the 'Spring Offensive' wage negotiations.

This is not always the case but it would still be most unusual to see placard-carrying union members behaving in an aggressive fashion. Usually, they continue to diligently perform their duties while wearing the armband symbolising protest. I was most amused to visit an ancient temple and read a sign in English which said 'Staff of this temple are on strike'. I could see no evidence of any inconvenience to the public as a result of this strike action.

Strikes are planned in advance and announced in the media to cause minimum disruption to customers. This seems little consolation to a commuter if a train strike brings the country to a grinding halt. However, one must remember that the number of days lost is minimal compared to the once-famed beer and airline strikes which could almost be predicted in Australia at most Christmas seasons.

It is common to have a union representative on the board of the company. This provides visible recognition that the future of workers is closely linked to the ultimate success of the company.

Once staff members are promoted to manager status, they are no longer eligible to be union representatives. Many have gone on to become presidents of the company! The chief executive officer of Fuji Bank is one such example. So is a former president of Mazda Motors, Kenichi Yamamoto, who joined the company as a graduate on the shop floor. In the course of working his way up through the ranks, he held the position of president of the Mazda employee union.

The Chairman of Sony, Akio Morita, claims that his company makes little distinction between blue- and white-collar workers when choosing future leaders: 'If a man or woman becomes successful as a union leader, we are very interested because these are the kind of people we are looking for in our management ranks'.

In some firms, it is actually a prerequisite to have been a union leader if you aspire to the managing director's position.

All union officers are elected by secret ballot.

It takes only a minimum of two people to start a union. If this occurs, employers have no option but to bargain with this legally-recognised body.

There is no nationwide minimum wage applied to all industries, although there are regional and industry minimums.

It's legal to dock salary if, for example, a person is even 10 minutes late for work. However, that is not a common practice—either to be late or to reduce pay accordingly.

The employer may be required to pay wages in advance, should the employee make this request in case of an emergency.

Unionised employees are officially hired to do a certain kind of work and cannot be transferred without their agreement. Therefore, don't expect a computer programmer to become a sales representative unless she is willing to do so. This is a challenge when balancing resources as a result of a shift in market demand or restructuring.

Enterprise union membership is not industry-wide but restricted to members of one company. Therefore, if workers lose their job, they also automatically relinquish their union affiliation; and nobody is available to help in a time when they might most need assistance.

Unions are predominantly found in large companies and the public service. Membership has constantly declined since the Second World War, when approximately 50 per cent of workers were union members. This figure was reduced to 33 per cent in 1977 and to 28.2 per cent in 1986.

In late 1987, the Japanese Private Sector Trade Union Confederation (Rengo) became the largest labour organisation, with a membership of 5.5 million people representing 62 labour unions. This accounts for 60 per cent of all private sector unionists. Only 28 per cent of private sector workers are unionised. The formation of Rengo was a prelude to the alliance of private and public sector unions and the dissolution of the General Council of Trade Unions (Sohyo), which was once the biggest national labour group. They were the prime group responsible for spearheading the annual wage negotiations each spring, as well as occasional campaigns against the government.

Thomas Nevins' *Labour Pains and the Gaijin Boss* is an excellent 300-page book which deals specifically with union and salary issues.

Refer also to: Allowances and benefits, Bonus, Communication . . . and useful phrases, Decisions, Hygiene factors, Lifelong employment, Obligation, Recruiting, Resignation and retrenchment, Salary, Service, Transfers, Work ethic

V

VACATIONS

The length of annual vacation varies with a person's age and length of service with the company. In addition to annual leave, there are many public holidays.

Most companies have policies which state employees cannot accumulate vacations for more than 12–24 months. Vacation days cannot be legally paid off in cash, although this sometimes occurs.

Most older Japanese in the work force do not regard holidays with the same zest as the average Western worker. One of my staff had many weeks of outstanding vacation which I kept encouraging him to take. But he relinquished over half of his allotment, stating he preferred to come to work. The stated rationale was that he could not afford to travel so he had no option but to stay home with a wife and noisy children in a small, steamy flat. This was seen as less preferable than coming to an air-conditioned office to interact with colleagues. He was the exception, rather than the rule!

This is definitely not the attitude of the new generation of worker, who is not as dedicated to the work ethic as those who felt the need to be so after the war. The younger staff member eagerly looks forward to vacations and has more disposable income with which to travel during that time.

The government has recently introduced a program to encourage companies to work only a five-day week and provide more leisure time. The norm of the office staff working every Saturday morning is changing rapidly. The majority of Japanese management support the notion of shorter working hours as long as it's not in their own company. Over 65 per cent of managers polled told the Japan Productivity Centre they feared the need to employ more staff, to maintain production, if hours are cut. But they also admitted that, in today's employment climate, they must offer shorter hours and more holidays to recruit high-quality staff.

Refer also to: Gift giving, Holidays and festivals, Work ethic

VISAS AND OTHER LEGAL DOCUMENTS

Before going to Japan, it is necessary to have a valid passport from your country and acquire a visa.

You may enter Japan on a single entry visa or multiple entry visa. Obviously, the latter is preferable. You may obtain visas for such purposes as investment, cultural, study etc., and the requirements for obtaining these different types of visas will vary. Don't assume a spouse will be able to automatically obtain a visa as well.

The regulations for obtaining a work visa also differ from country to country so be sure to check with the Japanese consulate in your home country before you depart. Make these arrangements well in advance, as it could take some time and will probably require a letter from an employer or other guarantor.

In some instances, you may require inoculations, although this has been relaxed in recent years.

Follow all the rules, however bureaucratic they may seem, as there is only one way to enter the country and that is *their* way!

All foreigners 16 years of age or older who take up residence in Japan must report to the local municipal office within 90 days of arrival. Here, you will obtain an alien registration certificate. This is every bit as important as your passport and must be carried at all times and presented to authorities on request. To obtain this certificate, go to your local town or ward office with your passport, Japanese address, black and white photograph (5 cm x 5 cm). Fill out an application form. If you plan to stay more than one year, your fingerprints will be taken. You will receive the certificate, which is good for five years' on the same day, but allow a couple of hours for this process. Any subsequent changes of address, name or employer must be recorded within 14 days.

If you have a baby, you should receive a birth record from the maternity ward at the hospital. Then report to the local town office and obtain an alien registration certificate for the child. Then report to your own consulate to determine what actions are required to obtain citizenship in your home country for the child. In order to travel with your offspring, report to a Japanese immigration office with the baby's and parents' passports, birth certificates and copy of a marriage licence. After filling out some more forms, you will receive a Japanese visa for the baby, stamped in the passport.

When you leave Japan, you are required to present your alien registration certificate, passport and boarding pass to immigration officials as well as your re-entry permit. If you do not have a re-entry permit, you will be required to surrender your alien registration certificate.

If you wish to extend your intended length of stay, you must apply at the immigration office prior to the expiry date. After many years of living in Japan, you may apply for permanent residence status if you meet stringent requirements.

Refer also to: Automobiles, Baggage, Legal matters, Medical, Pets, Salary, Tax

W

WOMEN

Japanese women epitomise femininity. Their petite figures, delicate movements and genteel demeanour always made me feel like an overgrown oaf by comparison.

Unfortunately, these commendable traits do not translate into success in the business world. If Japanese women are to be treated with any commercial respect, they must first refrain from bouts of nervous giggling, in which they place their hands over their mouths and appear to hide behind them. No amount of equal opportunity laws will better the business lot of women unless the individuals concerned act in a recognised business-like manner.

Discrimination against women in hiring and working conditions was first banned by the government in 1985. Since then, most companies have made some provision for women to follow previously male-dominated career paths.

There is still debate whether women are their own worst enemies and do not, in fact, wish to seriously pursue careers. There remains an assumption that a young woman would only join a company to find a husband. Although many do marry colleagues they meet at work and resign immediately, it must be remembered that others have ambitions to become company directors.

Choice must be the key factor. Some married women return to work after raising children but many find they do not have ample time to do justice to domestic demands as well as a job. Many Western career women struggle with the same thing but the concept of 'superwoman', who successfully balances both career and family, is still a rarity in Japan.

Equal opportunity legislation was officially introduced in April 1986 but the reality is that women are still rarely found in management ranks. This too is changing as companies recognise the enormous wealth of talent among half the population, but changing rather slowly. There seems little vocal public sentiment for these changes to occur more quickly, in spite of the establishment of a government department to improve the status of women and produce statistics on the increase of women in professional positions.

I personally know of one woman with a PhD in physics who could only obtain a job as a secretary; and have heard of many similar unfortunate instances. One young woman, working in my department, had a Masters degree in literature from Columbia University. She was an extremely talented and conscientious worker. When a first-line management position arose, I suggested her manager appoint her to that role. He was supportive, against strong opposition from all other male colleagues. We were informed that we were putting her in a position to fail. I knew it wouldn't be easy for her so we had a chat about the harsh reality of those difficulties. I asked her to seriously consider whether she wanted to take on the job, knowing the likely opposition. She took the position. She struggled at first. She had self-doubt and needless opposition to plans she wanted to implement. She persevered. The last I heard, she had been promoted *again*.

Foreign females are generally more readily accepted than Japanese women in managerial roles. This is particularly true if they are mature and have a successful track record. They are also seen as a novelty, which can actually work in their favour.

Before I went to Japan, my boss indicated that, as a woman, I would probably have difficulty with the Japanese men I worked with. He anticipated personnel issues with the men reporting directly to me, but thought I should accept the position, regardless. To make matters worse, I was younger than any of them. With that vote of confidence, I approached the situation with some fear and trepidation. That probably wasn't a bad idea, rather than assuming the normal air of confidence I would feign in a strange Western environment.

I initially indicated to the male managers reporting to me that I would need to rely on their expertise. I asked them to help educate me so we could work together as a team.

There was, admittedly, a somewhat uneasy breaking-in period for all concerned. I attempted to 'keep my receiver on high and my transmitter on low' and solicit their views, rather than impose my own. As the weeks and months passed, more direct and open communication developed. We gradually felt easier. We didn't mention the obvious fact that I was a woman. Maybe my managers did have a problem with it, but if that was the case, they were kind enough never to make it apparent to me. I can only say they were as fine a group of individuals as anyone could ever hope to work with. I could not have wished for a more cooperative or dedicated team.

The situation could easily have differed, depending on the individuals concerned and the attitude of higher management toward competence, regardless of sex.

I recognise it would have been much easier for me working with Japanese in an American company than a woman working in a Japanese company. I also realise it was easier for me, as a Western woman, than it would have been for a Japanese woman. However, times are changing, albeit slowly, and there are increasing numbers of very talented Japanese women being promoted to managerial positions.

Still, not many women achieve top jobs. Among 750 career diplomats, only 20 are female. Likewise, less than 1 per cent of management-level government bureaucrats are female (*Time* magazine, 23 October 1989).

In spite of the fact that more women graduate from college than men, a proportionate number are not given meaningful career paths in major Japanese firms. This is also changing as companies slowly realise they are missing out on the skills of talented students.

The role of women is changing in Japan and will continue to do so. When I lived there, no one would have dreamed that a female would become leader of a major political party. In 1989, Takako Doi did just that. I asked my Japanese friends if that had a major impact on aspirations of other women. The response is mixed. Some say yes, while others believe she was just a token and there has been no change in attitude as a result of her high public profile. Who knows? But there can be little argument that this unexpected occurrence must have some impact on the aspirations of younger women.

In July 1989, there was a record of 22 successful females

in the July elections for the Diet's Upper House. 'Nearly 50 per cent of women work outside the home but sexual stereotyping and continuing unofficial discrimination hold most of them back' (*Time* magazine, 23 October 1989).

I know this statement to be true but try to refrain from undue criticism of stereotyped jobs because I found it strange that golf clubs had female caddies. I always felt uncomfortable having another female carry my clubs. You see, I'd bought into the Western stereotype that physical labour was 'man's work'.

Still, Japanese women who are not satisfied to be housewives must overcome attitudes embedded in the culture. According to a 1987 government survey, more than one-third of women and half of men believed a man's place was at work and a woman's in the home.

The average salary for women working full time is 60 per cent that of men. One-fourth of Japanese women have part-time jobs to increase their disposable income.

Sexual harassment is not an issue which is widely discussed in human resource circles. In less progressive companies, there is an unwritten code that insinuates a manager may take certain liberties with his female employees. As long as no one complains—no one cares.

Sexual harassment has been quite widespread but seldom talked about because women were reluctant to complain. That is no longer the case. There has been much publicity about lawsuits filed against offending bosses and some lawyers are even offering telephone counselling on the subject. However, much of the media trivialises the situation by making jokes about women.

The concept of sexual harassment is quite novel in Japan and only recently gained public recognition as an issue. Apparently, some striptease clubs have established special *sekihara* areas where women playing the part of office workers can be fondled by customers, who are no longer supposed to engage in such activity in the workplace.

There is an inbuilt temptation for Western men on assignment in Japan to be infatuated with the Japanese women he meets. The secretaries are extremely attentive and almost revere the ground on which the boss walks. In their desire to please, it would be easy to exceed the normal bounds of a working relationship. It is not for me to moralise on this issue as every situation is different but prudence would be a good maxim to follow. I know of one American executive who was fired from his New York-based office for 'overenthusiastic' affiliations with office staff. But I also know of another who is now happily married to his former secretary.

Before the war, Japanese women who chose to marry foreigners lost their citizenship. There is still some disdain about intermarriage, although many more are occurring. It is said that the name of Yoko Ono (John Lennon's widow) is often written in the *katakana* alphabet, the equivalent of writing a Western name in lower case letters to signify lesser importance.

In late 1990, the Ministry of Labour launched its first job-training program for Tokyo housewives and plans to expand the program nationally in 1991.

Labour-intensive retail stores are doing their best to woo women back to the work force in a market which is experiencing a severe labour shortage. Isetan department stores have introduced trend-setting maternity benefits with flexible working hours to attract young mothers back behind the counter. Keio, another large retailer, allows part-timers to chose their own shifts as long as they put in at least five hours, three days a week (*Tomodachi*, May 1991).

In her book *Women Executives in Japan*, Yuriko Saisho states that women don't seem to be very good at helping each other and often tend to bring other women down. This may not be so different from many Western women, although networking support seems to be more widespread. But certainly Japan provides an extreme case of lack of support when Saisho states: 'Many Japanese mothers complain when their sons' schoolteachers are women. These mothers do not trust other women.'

This is somewhat ironic, in that most Japanese men entrust their entire pay packets to the female of the household. But that has always been socially acceptable. It will take time before women acquire power outside the domestic scene.

Real power, versus perceived improvements, will take longer still. Japan's military illustrates the point. Over 2 per cent of Japan's defence forces are female. Yet they still learn the traditional bridal skill of flower arranging as part of their training (*National Geographic,* April 1990).

I am often asked if the plight of the Japanese woman is really that much different from the inequality which still exists to varying degrees in Western countries. I can only reply that my assessment is totally subjective, but if I was to write a report card and grade the acceptance of women in the workplace, I would give the following ratings:

B+ Scandinavia (no personal experience—only what I've read)

B United States and Canada

C Australia

D Japan

These are not percentages but relative rankings. Admittedly, they are overgeneralisations (which I keep saying one mustn't do!).

I must also confess that I have personally never been a victim of sexual discrimination in any of the countries in which I have worked. I have been fortunate to have had the opportunity to work with enlightened management. One of the greatest joys of my stay in Japan was serving as a mentor to some extremely talented young women and seeing the pleasing results when they were encouraged to stretch their traditional workplace limitations.

Refer also to: Discretion . . . and loss of face, Entertainment, Recruiting, Temporaries, Tradition, Unions

WORK ETHIC

Are the Japanese really workaholics?

It's safe to say that, on average, they put in longer hours than the ordinary office worker in the West. However, 'work' may be defined as early morning company exercise sessions or having drinks after hours with colleagues or clients. There remains a notion that if a worker arrives home at an early hour, they must not have an important job. Likewise, it is still common to wait until the boss has departed before you leave the office. But both these practices are changing and younger employees will quite candidly state (at least to a Westerner) they would rather be doing such recreational activities as swimming, aerobics or dancing.

It is important for a Western manager to understand these changes. I was a slow learner. I was near exhaustion after three weeks of working until 9.00 or 10.00 p.m. for fear of being regarded as a lazy Westerner (after reading so much about the hard-working Japanese). One evening, a senior member of staff hesitantly approached me and respectfully stated: 'DeVrye-*san* . . . we are worried that you work too hard'.

I explained that I didn't wish to be regarded as a lazy Westerner and wanted to work as hard as my team so we were all proud of each other. After much tentative discussion, it finally dawned on my thick *gaijin* brain that my staff were only at the office because I was still present.

Worse still, they were not necessarily engaged in productive activity but simply felt it mandatory to remain until the boss departed. What a relief to understand the waiting game. I immediately changed my work pattern and left the premises around 7.00 p.m., finishing off any loose ends at home.

Here was a situation where both employer and employee thought they were doing the right thing by the other. In fact, through misunderstanding, both were unhappy. How much easier if we hadn't bought into the traditional stereotypes and simply discussed it openly at an earlier stage, rather than assume what expectations the other party had of the work ethic.

Other working environments most certainly generated different expectations. A friend in the marketing department of a computer company informed me her boss told her to have an early night and take the last train home! For the previous three weeks, they had been working until 3.00 or 4.00 a.m. When I asked how it was possible to maintain productivity, she admitted they really weren't that effective. As a result, colleagues were slumped asleep at their desks during normal daylight hours. However, they wanted to give the customer the impression that they were always there, working through the night to install the computer. One can't help but wonder if the customer may have also been dozing at that time of the morning!

I have Japanese friends working in Australia and the United States who wouldn't dream of leaving work before 8.00 p.m. and others who can't wait until the traditional closure at 5.00 p.m. However, I also know hundreds of professional Westerners with exactly the same range of dedication.

There is one difference. It would be unusual for non-management staff in Western companies to willingly work overtime as a matter of course, whereas I've often called Japanese firms in Australia after 6.00 p.m. and been surprised that a receptionist was still present to answer the call.

The Japanese are working less. The number of hours spent at work, excluding public holidays and annual vacation, declined from 203 hours per month in 1960 to 175 hours per month in 1986. This averages approximately 43.75 hours per week. According to the latest figures from the Ministry of Labour, the Japanese worked an average of 2111 hours per year in 1988 and 2016 hours in 1991. On an annual basis, it is nearly 200 hours more than Britain and the United States; and 500 more than France and West Germany (*Tomodachi*, February 1991). According to the *Japan Almanac*, as reported in the *Asahi Shimbun*, the Japanese government had set a target to reduce the number of annual hours to 1800 by 1993 but was reported as unlikely to meet that reduction in working hours.

As an aside . . . these figures were compiled before the days of mobile phones which are now an integral part of working life in Japan, just as Japan was one of the first countries in the world to fully utilise the fax machine. Does time spent on the mobile phone on the way home now constitute work time?

The astronomically high price of real estate has driven younger people further from the city and increased their commuting time. The average commuting time for our office staff was one and three-quarter hours *each* way. Logic dictates this can only motivate a work force to spend fewer actual hours in the office.

The older generation had no choice but to rebuild Japan after the war. Today's youth have no such pressing necessity or sense of obligation. They are rapidly becoming the definitive 'yuppies'. As a result, Korea and Taiwan are becoming increasingly competitive, with lower wage rates and still the desire to improve their personal lifestyles, as well as the national economy.

I had the opportunity to hear Professor Michael Yoshino of Harvard Business School describe a conversation he had with a client who was chief executive of a large company in Japan. As Professor Yoshino was consulting with the firm, the president complained: 'Young people just don't want to work so hard'. Upon further investigation, the Harvard academic discovered the youth referred to by the 82-year-old president, were, in fact, the 65-year-old vice presidents!

To many Japanese men in their fifties and sixties, work has been the primary reason for their existence and one and the same as leisure. Life without work would be a meaningless experience and leisure was simply regarded as a necessity to rest before work commenced again. This is no longer the case and young people actively plan their leisure time. Again, be careful not to overgeneralise as there are still young people who would be classed as workaholics and older people who enjoy hobbies more than work.

I met a man in his mid-fifties who was a professor at

one of the leading universities in Tokyo. He openly admitted that he preferred golf, photography and reading Chaucer to teaching, and only worked because he needed the money to pursue his leisure interests.

It is far too easy a rationalisation for Westerners to say that overworked staff would rather be at work than home with their families or friends.

In 1986, the Japanese government formed a committee to encourage citizens to work a shorter week but the committee, itself, ended up working six days a week! After a year, it had reached no solution and was disbanded.

Most large Japanese firms have adopted the five-day week but this has not filtered down to smaller organisations. The difference between small and large companies is marked and those in smaller companies almost always work much longer hours.

By 1984, half of all Japanese companies had adopted 'some kind of two-day weekend' policy. However, that didn't mean giving employees every weekend off. More likely, it would consist of 1–2 weekends per month. Even then, staff may be required to work extra hours during the week which doesn't, in reality, reduce their available leisure time.

It should also be remembered that there could be ulterior motives for working long hours. Until a young college graduate reaches the level of *kanri shoku* (middle management), he or she is paid overtime and the household budget may rely on an overtime cheque. This could account for nearly 15 per cent of annual income, which is not insignificant.

There must be an agreement with the majority of workers before overtime can be 'assigned'. There is no legal limit on overtime for adult males and the rates must be at least 25 per cent of the wage.

At one stage, women could only work 150 overtime hours a year. Mothers were required to take five months maternity leave whether they wanted to or not.

There is some train of thought among established companies in Japan that foreign firms 'spoil' Japanese employees. They believe this is the case in instances when the overseas company is not fully familiar with local practice or does not know the legal basis of obligation. It is surmised they subsequently allow employees the luxury of working less hours than their counterparts in other companies who also realise this discrepancy.

There is no doubt some truth in this statement. However, as personnel manager for an American company, I discovered a rather unique workload problem within weeks of my arrival. The 'problem' was not that management thought everyone wasn't working hard enough. Rather, it was felt they were working too hard and possibly not making the best decisions, as a result of burnout. There was great debate in various sectors of the organisation whether this was or wasn't a problem. Once the chief executive defined it as such, my task was to put together a strategy to address the workload issue, without any resulting loss of productivity.

With a background in recreation, I attacked this unique problem with great zeal, formulating a plan to have people make more use of leisure time. Then it hit me. About 10.30 p.m. one Friday night, as I was glued to my computer screen, devising this blueprint, I burst out in uncontrollable laughter. Any minute now, someone would walk in and take me away in a straitjacket. How ironic that on a Friday night, here was me, myself, I . . . actually *working* on a proposal to get people to work less! I'm not quite sure what the moral of this story is other than that it's entirely true; and it's sometimes easy to get things somewhat out of perspective—whether in Japan or any other strange environment.

One of the strategies to reduce workload was to introduce home computer terminals. What a great idea . . . employees could now be linked up to the head office in New York 24 hours a day, seven days a week!

As cynical as I originally was, I had to admit this was indeed useful to allow communication in 'real time' with New York. It meant that employees could return home and have dinner with the family. Then, *if* they wanted, they could later sign on to the electronic network which would transmit and receive messages across the world in a matter of seconds.

There were certainly benefits across time zones if you were able to manage the system rather than allow it to manage you. At first, this was difficult as it seemed the screen, like a ringing phone or letter box, drew you to it just to see if anything important was happening. However, after a few weeks, I was able to turn it on only if I was expecting something important. I readily acquired enough discipline not to 'open' the mail if it was sent from someone I knew would probably only generate work and expect a response at midnight.

However, as personnel manager, I had to react quickly if

there were real emergencies at any hour. On more than one occasion, I received urgent phone calls in the middle of the night, informing me of the death of a member of the employee's family back home, and would then make the necessary arrangements for the employee to return.

As Japan continues on the road to economic prosperity, many traditional industries are finding it difficult to attract younger people to do the jobs. Many of today's youth do not want to engage in activity which is considered too dirty, too smelly or too strenuous. This has resulted in a number of employers utilising foreign workers from India, Pakistan or the Philippines who are quite grateful to earn in excess of US$100 per day for such manual work. Although it is illegal to use such workers, many small factories claim they have no choice if they wish to continue producing goods at a competitive price; or even staying in production at all.

Many of these illegal workers may only stay in Japan for a short period of time before returning to their home country with a large volume of cash savings, which would otherwise take a lifetime to earn in a poorer nation. It would appear that entire families arrive in the country. In a case which attracted media headlines, a 12-year-old Pakistani boy was tangled and killed in a machine. When there was an investigation into why an underage, illegal immigrant was working, the government washed its hands of all responsibility. The authorities claimed they had no obligation to the family for compensation because the person shouldn't have been there in the first place. The factory concerned, surprisingly, received no retribution.

Japan has very strict immigration laws so where do these workers come from? They are procured by brokers who have an elaborate network of contacts in both the Japanese and overseas governments. These so called brokers are quite probably linked to the *Yakuza*, who are, in essence, the Japanese mafia.

The work ethic extends to more than simply the number of hours worked. There is an unstated, yet expected, loyalty to the organisation and requirements to adhere to the codes of conduct even after working hours.

I spent a few days with a delightful schoolteacher in Imabare—a small fishing town on the island of Shikoku. She was an extremely cautious driver and explained that she would not only incur a fine if she was caught speeding, but would probably get a pay deduction or be denied a future salary increase. If she was charged with drink driving, she would be asked to resign from her job. Very simply, a person of her standing in the small community was expected to always set a good example for youth.

Refer also to: Allowances and benefits, Bonus, Education and training, Entertainment, Holidays and festivals, Lunches, Lifelong employment, Obligation, Quality, Recruiting, Service, Tradition, Unions, Vacations

X

X-PATS

Japan was once an island nation isolated from the world. Today, the influx of expatriates into most segments of the country is the norm. However, each time you re-enter the country and stand in an airport queue to pass through the turnstile labelled 'Aliens', you are gently reminded that you are not quite an integral part of this once homogeneous population. This is no real barrier to success.

In the Orient or anywhere else, you will only be successful at doing business if people like you. They will like you if you make a genuine effort to understand *their* perspective and attempt to fit into *their* country. Just think how condemning we are of newcomers to our country who make no attempt to learn the language or assimilate into the general community.

There are some companies which have been established specifically to help foreigners settle into Japan. These organisations will not only assist with the legal requirements but be available for a whole range of other services. These could range from house-hunting to enrolling children in school to taking spouses grocery-shopping. The spectrum of services varies. Naturally, so do the charges, depending on the degree of assistance required. My personal view is that the money is well spent to help save time through the initial hassles of obtaining alien registrations and driver's certificates. I seriously question whether it is necessary to pay to have someone take you grocery shopping.

Expats and their families should be carefully selected. They should be flexible, sensitive and above all, tolerant, if they are to be good ambassadors for your company. Some firms go to the extent of providing pre-assignment psychological counselling to assess both the employee and partner for their attitudes in this regard. I'm not sure if it is necessary to go to this degree. It certainly is imperative, before offering a firm commitment of an assignment, that the individuals concerned are told of both the pros *and* cons of accepting the move.

It is important that people like you if they are to do business with you. It is difficult to warm to any individual who complains about your country.

For the first six months I lived in Japan, I was quite convinced there were not, indeed, 24 hours in a day. I never had enough time to take care of the basics of life. It seemed to take an inordinately long period of time to get a haircut, buy a light globe, arrange theatre tickets etc. This was in no way the fault of Japanese efficiency. It was simply that I couldn't readily detect signs offering such services and was thereby confronted with the language 'problem'. This caused enormous frustration until I realised that it was *my* problem.

I became very adept at charades and outwardly smiled a lot. Inwardly, I was often churning with anxiety. I kept telling myself to focus on the positive and not let the 'little' things get to me, but it was the minor irritations which caused the most frustration. At this point, I must confess that I hated my first three months in Japan. It was not easy. My phone bill home was outrageous. The next three months were somewhat better. By the end of the first year, I was quite comfortable. And, at the end of the second year, I didn't want to leave. Hang in there!

You interact with a lot of nationalities, other than Japanese, in the very cosmopolitan environment of Tokyo. I never ceased to be amazed at how frequently I bumped into other expatriates I knew, in a city of 20 million people. If analysed, it wasn't all that extraordinary because we tended to frequent certain areas. Also, as Westerners, we literally 'stood out' (usually a few inches higher) in a crowd. Still, I would be surprised that a number of people, whom I hadn't seen, would comment: 'Oh, I noticed you at such and such a place last weekend'. With this higher-than-normal public profile, it is important that expatriates act with the utmost discretion and politeness at all times.

Unfortunately, I encountered some who were anything but good ambassadors for their company and country. The most extreme example occurred at 10.00 p.m. one evening as I was unwinding in a bath. The phone rang and the spouse of one of our assignees demanded: 'Could you please have one of the Japs come over to change a light bulb'.

This occurred very early in my tenure. I was almost speechless but politely informed her it wasn't my department's responsibility and she should change it herself, just as she would do at home. She became most irate and stated that if she was in her home country, her husband would do it but he was on a business trip and she didn't know how to do it in Japan so insisted it was, therefore, my role. Had this happy event occurred once I was more comfortable in my own job, I would have been tempted to tell her to test the connection by putting a wet finger in the socket!

Rather than that, I patiently explained how to remove a light bulb from a socket and outlined the difference between screw and bayonet fittings. I then gave an impromptu lesson on how to play charades with someone at a hardware store. This simply consisted of taking the globe into the store, pointing at it and smiling so the proprietor would sell you an identical replacement. Even I was amazed at my tolerance toward this moronic woman but guess I must have acquired a little more patience as a result of living in Japan. I still couldn't help but shake my head and ask for days after: 'Why are people like this allowed on international assignment as ambassadors for their company and country?'.

Sometimes, I felt like I was the complaints officer on the *Titanic* but the vast majority of assignees responsibly handled their own affairs as a normal part of the challenge of living in any strange environment.

I knew of a few spouses who refused to visit a restaurant unless it had been verified as having a 'Western' toilet. They constantly carried a camping knife and fork in their handbag so they wouldn't need to use chopsticks. As a host, I would personally find this outward display of inflexibility somewhat offensive. However, as much as I preach adaptation to local norms, I must confess I always tried to discreetly carry a couple of muesli or granola bars with me if I was staying overnight in a local Japanese inn, as I never quite got used to facing fish and raw eggs for breakfast.

I never ceased to be amazed that otherwise capable and intelligent expats could engage in hours of trivial conversation complaining about life in Japan. Entire dinner parties could focus on an overcrowded shrine during festival time; or complaints about the size of one's kitchen; or how much one spent on shopping expeditions.

Admittedly, it's impossible to leave all emotional baggage behind in your home country. It's understandable to worry about sick and ageing parents, estranged children living with a former spouse whom you can't have ready weekend access to if you're 10 000 kilometres away, and pets who don't comprehend why their owner is no longer present.

Expatriates in any country are generally perceived by the locals as needlessly wealthy creatures, who assume an arrogant presence and are of questionable value. That is why it is important to win the respect of your fellow workers in a demonstrable area of expertise which is not available locally. It is also important to be sensitive to their salary and benefits, and not flaunt the perks of your expat package.

A normal expat package would not only include an excellent salary but make generous provision for a cost-of-living allowance. More significantly, expats and their families are usually provided with luxurious (by Japanese standards) accommodation in the most prestigious suburbs. This is usually near the office, whereas the average commuting time for the Tokyo office worker is an hour and forty minutes each way.

Expats may also receive membership in the American Club or other facilities which are outside the budget of the average employee in Japan. This can create some resentment, especially if two people are doing similar jobs and only one is on an expat package. The discontent can be increased if the foreigner still complains that the apparently luxurious apartment doesn't compare with their half-acre in Connecticut.

Most expat packages allow for a trip home every one or two years. This is seen as a big benefit by the Japanese. They see the foreigner and family escaping the humidity of a Tokyo summer for a month, whereas the average Japanese worker could not contemplate taking his family overseas, especially for such a protracted period.

At this stage, I must be careful to emphasise the considerable difference between a person on an expat package, compared to a struggling student teaching English or a Westerner who has independently found employment in a Japanese company. There are definitely different classes of foreign workers in Japan. When I refer to expatriates, I mean those who are on temporary assignment from their home companies.

It would be ideal to give some of these assignees greed inoculations to help combat their conspicuous consumption. However, almost the same applies to Japanese expatriates living abroad. They are perceived by Americans, Australians and British colleagues to have substantially more 'perks' than the locals. There is also expressed resentment that they have much greater influence with head office, so are therefore viewed with some suspicion. I emphasise this so I am not accused of attacking only the expatriate Westerner.

Having said this, I must confess that I had more trouble adapting to the American executives I met than I did adjusting to the Japanese way of doing business. Not to be misinterpreted . . . I very much enjoy the company of Americans and some of my best friends are citizens of the

United States. It was simply that I arrived in Japan with certain expectations. I expected Japanese to be different and adapted accordingly. I made the mistake of not anticipating people with the same language and skin colour as myself to have a different approach to business proceedings than Australians. But, that's an entirely different subject. It's just that I used to get annoyed when overhearing someone complain they couldn't get proper 'American' cup of coffee. How indignant would we be if a tourist loudly demanded a 'Japanese' cup of tea in a Madison Avenue restaurant?

The American Club had one of the best facilities in Tokyo. More is said about that in the entry on Sport and recreation. As useful as the club is, it is a mistake to centre all social activities around that establishment. One could easily be misled to believe you would be experiencing the 'real' Japan if you simply went on tours organised by the club. The American Club is undoubtedly a pleasant haven to see a movie in English or have a Western meal. But those who confine the majority of their social activities there may become insular and miss out on what is really happening in Japan.

There is a new breed of *gaijin* who would not be likely to fall into that trap. This new generation of foreigners are usually young and fluent in Japanese. They may even have been educated in Japan as the offspring of a former expat. At that stage, they were young enough to be receptive to the cultural differences. As they enter the world of business, they have fewer preconceived notions of what it 'ought' to be like to deal with the Japanese. They have not bought into stereotypes and can readily adapt to the circumstances at hand.

Each expatriate community has its old hands. These are individuals who have been around for some time and see themselves somewhat above those who come and go on short-term assignments. There is a certain old-boys' network of those who have lived abroad for many years and they treat newcomers or short-timers in a different way. That is not to say they cannot be extremely helpful in providing advice, but old hands have their own more intimate circles.

Intimacy takes on a different meaning for the expat. There is a lot of coming and going of assignees so don't be surprised if someone describes a close friend as someone they have known for more than two months!

Soon after I had arrived in Tokyo, I met a woman with whom I thought I would have quite a bit in common. I made this comment to another acquaintance and received the amazing reply: 'Don't waste your time getting to know her because she's leaving in a few weeks'. I instantly was on the defensive and countered with, 'All the more reason to get to know her in a hurry before the opportunity passes'.

I still think there is some truth in my naive reply. However, I was later to admit that in the expat environment, you often have no past with people you meet and are unlikely to see them in the future. In instances where you do meet up in another country, you may find you have nothing in common other than your previous life in Japan. Again, this is a gross overgeneralisation—I must stop breaking my own rules!

But that philosophy, which is adopted by many, helps explain why you may not receive automatic invitations to dinner parties or other expatriates may not reciprocate in the same way you would anticipate.

That is also why it is important to initially seek out those of similar interests, without worrying whether it is the 'right' thing to do. Some colleagues were amazed that I was 'brave enough' to play squash with a senior vice president who was a number of levels higher on the corporate totem pole and revered by all in our office. In a New York environment, he would more likely have fraternised with peers but we were about the same athletic standard and enjoyed the workout. I also think it may be even more lonely at the top for executives away from head office for a relatively short period of time.

I believe IBM made an error by only posting assignees for an average period of two years. That allows for little continuity, particularly in management ranks. Many others echoed the sentiment that by the time they learned enough to become truly effective at work, it was almost time to return. Considering the expense of transferring an expatriate family and reduced productivity during a settling-in phase, the minimum stay should be three years. Five would be preferable.

Anytime there is a change in leaders at the top of an organisation, it is important to retain consistency of management. Therefore, it is ideal if there can be a hand-over period of 2–3 months to allow for a smooth transition and familiarisation. Yes, it is an added expense to support two expat families but certainly a worthwhile investment, especially if it is the chief executive officer.

The most important thing for an expat to remember is to be yourself and treat every person you meet in Japan as an individual. Be consistent in your management style. Do not overgeneralise and interact with all Japanese in the same manner, any more than you would treat every Westerner in an identical fashion. Remember, every book you read about the Japanese (or any other nation) is simply a collection of observations concerning trends. People all over the world are individuals . . . with individual foibles, interests and hot buttons.

The way in which a foreign manager can earn respect is by demonstrating that they add tangible value to the company team. It also helps if a *gaijin* is perceived as making an effort to understand the local culture. Naturally, familiarity with the language is a big plus but even for those with limited linguistic skills, it helps to learn a few words such as hello, thank you, sorry, keep up the good work etc.

Regardless of how adaptable you may be, there will always be times of frustrations in a strange land. Just make sure the good times far outnumber the bad . . . whether you're in your home country or a visitor in another.

Refer also to: Every other chapter, especially Communication . . . and useful phrases, Names

Y

YES

The important thing to remember is that 'yes' does not mean 'yes'. It simply indicates that the other party has understood what you have said. It does not for a moment imply they agree with you.

Refer also to: Communication . . . and useful phrases, Decisions, Meetings

YOUTH

Shinjinrui refers to the new generation. Over 50 per cent of today's Japanese population were born after the Second World War.

This generation of Japanese entering the work force have known no hardship. They see no need to be as 'hungry' or dedicated as their parents. They are more the 'me' generation who have only experienced affluence in their lifetime. They are the future of the work force.

Some may wish to work for only a couple of years and then, having accumulated enough cash, leave the company and possibly the country to travel abroad and experience the rest of the world first-hand, a world which fascinates Japanese every bit as much, if not more, than the fascination we hold for their country.

Most resignations of this sort will usually occur just after a bonus payment in June or December. I don't have any statistics but it appears the urge to travel beyond one's own borders could be likened to Australian youth of the 1960s and 1970s, who made a 'compulsory' sojourn to the United Kingdom for a year or so; and the Americans who hitched around Europe after high school or university. Until recently, the Japanese did not have this luxury. Now, they are travelling more extensively, at a time when Western youth seem more conservative and conscious of finding longer-term careers.

Much emphasis is placed on educating Japan's youth

and the country boasts one of the highest percentages of high school retention in the world. Even at junior high school level, there is intense competition for places in the better schools. Entrance to top high schools leads to places in more prestigious universities, which ultimately leads to better jobs and higher pay.

In 1950, only 1 per cent of new entrants in the labour force attended institutes of higher learning. In 1980, this figure was over 40 per cent and growing. The high school graduate is unlikely ever to exceed the salary of the university graduate and this gulf widens with age.

Many of the more affluent Japanese send their children overseas for a year to attend a foreign high school or university. This group may develop the same ambitious attitudes of their Western contemporaries and become frustrated upon entering a traditional Japanese company, where they would not reap the financial rewards of their education until at least their mid thirties. Meanwhile, they see their overseas counterparts become affluent yuppies in more prestigious positions. Traditional Japanese management style is less likely to give young 'high fliers' much responsibility to develop new opportunities. However, *if* given the opportunity, they respond with a great deal of initiative.

Younger people in business are concerned with many of the same issues which confront management globally. For example, there is a greater awareness of the need to protect the environment, which is having enormous impact on the once elaborate packaging of Japanese goods.

Professor Michael Yoshino of Harvard University

believes young employees, the world over, need to become more global in their outlook to succeed in the future. In an address to Australian business in April 1991, he quoted both the chairmen of IBM and Sony as stating their number-one challenge was to become more global. It seemed strange that two recognised worldwide leaders in multinational firms would emphasise the need to instil a culture which encourages employees no longer to think of them as 'Japanese' or 'American' firms, but truly international. This will not happen overnight.

Following in the footsteps of one's father was once a strong tradition in Japan and is still evident in some occupations. This seems to be the case in politics, where it is estimated that 40 per cent of ruling party candidates for the Lower House are children of Diet members. As astounding as this figure sounds, it is probably not representative of the general trend in the work force (*Time* magazine, 19 February 1990 p. 38).

As well as mentioning Japanese youth, it is worthwhile to include information on young Westerners who work in Japan. Some may arrive independently after university to seek employment in a Japanese firm. More frequently, they have affiliations with international organisations such as AISEC, which arranges work experience exchanges for business graduates throughout the world.

IBM had a policy of hiring foreign students who were pursuing international studies. They were often employed as summer students or for one-year assignments. They were responsible for obtaining their own visas etc. and assigned project work. At first, there were mixed feelings about the cost–benefit to the organisation and a concern that students would eat up much valuable time of already busy employees, who would need to divert their energies to training these 'kids'.

My personal experience was they were an incredible asset to the business. For the most part, they were much more flexible than assignees. They did not receive, nor expect, all the benefits so were a fraction of the cost of an expatriate. And most had some previous training in international business which few full-time employees had experienced. The students I met were, without exception, highly-motivated, ambitious and skilled individuals who approached any task with great enthusiasm. They looked for ways to get around problems, rather than excuses why it couldn't be done. They injected a freshness into the organisation; and managers who utilised them effectively and provided them with challenging tasks (i.e. not photocopying) were rewarded for their efforts.

Refer also to: Bowing, Communication . . . and useful phrases, Education and training, Lifelong employment, Recruiting, Seniority, Work ethic

Z

ZAIBATSU

The *zaibatsu* were huge trading companies controlled by a handful of powerful Japanese families. Before the Second World War, they dominated much of Japan's major industry in a monopolistic fashion. They were ordered to dissolve during the Occupation and free enterprise was encouraged. However, these great companies still exist and are the key business leaders. Nonetheless, some outsiders like Honda and Panasonic have most certainly broken the monopoly situation. Japan now has one of the most even distributions of wealth of any country in the world.

Refer also to: Lifelong employment, Recruiting

ZILLION

There remain at least a zillion things yet to learn about how Japan works.

There are over 2000 *kanji* characters in one Japanese alphabet and no less than three such alphabets. That is still not enough to cover the variety of situations which you may encounter. In this book, I have relied on a meagre 26 characters in the English language to assist with a basic understanding of this complex and fascinating culture.

All individuals in any organisation have a learning curve, whether establishing operations in Tokyo, Sydney, London or New York. It's the successful ones who learn most quickly. As I admitted in the opening chapter, my own learning curve was so steep, there were times I longed for the safety rope of a mountaineer. Life in Japan was a juxtaposition of pleasure and frustration. Change was the only constant.

After two years in Japan, I sometimes forgot I was 'different' and was surprised when people approached me out of curiosity or to practise their English. I sometimes felt part Japanese. I occasionally believed I blended into the environment but unlike a chameleon, I had been distinctly unsuccessful. But I certainly felt more comfortable than when I arrived. When it came time to leave, I didn't want to go. Could this be the same person who, 18 months earlier, would gladly have taken the first flight out of Narita airport? I had learned a lot. I had made a lot of mistakes in that process, but life was now much easier . . . more comfortable.

The most important thing to remember is that there are more similarities than differences between Japan and the West. This is mainly because there are more similarities than differences among human beings. The biggest error would be to over-generalise about individuals or management styles operative in Japan. All people are diverse. There is no one Japanese way of doing things. Never let anyone get away with 'You don't really understand Japanese practice'.

Practices change!

Simply recognise there is more than one way to run a business. Glean as much information as you can from as many books and courses as you like, but the bottom line is your face-to-face interaction with other human beings with the same feelings, hopes and aspirations. Your own success ultimately comes down to personal judgement, based on what is the right thing to do at that point in time.

Learn from the past. Obtain information about the present but make your own decisions for the future direction of your enterprise.

I don't expect you to agree with everything you have read in this book. In fact, it would be disappointing if you did because if I've said it once, I've said it a thousand times, but this will be the last time in print for now . . . *remember to treat each situation and individual uniquely!*

My mission was to transfer skills and knowledge. I received far more than I ever gave. I would like to thank my colleagues in Japan for their understanding and kindness while they gently taught me not to believe everything I'd read. Through their patience, I gradually learned to use such information only as a guide to making business decisions, judgement which could only be sound if based on the circumstances of individual situations.

Similarly, one should use the material contained in this book unlike a drunk uses a lamp post . . . Use it only for illumination, not support! Your own judgement is the only factor on which you can constantly rely in the dynamic environment of business throughout the world.

In conclusion, there is only one thing left to say . . . *'Gambatte!'*. It's one of those marvellous Japanese sayings, which, roughly translated, simultaneously means . . . ***Do your best and Good luck!***

REFERENCES

Abegglen, J. and Stalk Jr. G., *Kaisha: The Japanese Corporation*, Basic Books, New York, 1985

American Chamber of Commerce in Japan, *Living in Japan*, Ogishima Graphics, Tokyo, 1983

Benedict, R., *The Chrysanthemum and the Sword. Patterns of Japanese Culture*, Tuttle, Tokyo, 1974

Bassin, G., *The Tokyo Transit Book*, The Japan Times Ltd, Tokyo, 1983

Christopher, R., *Second to None—American Companies in Japan*, Tuttle, Tokyo, 1986

Collins, R., *Max Danger—Adventures of an Expat in Tokyo*, Tuttle, Japan, 1987

Connor, J. and Yoshida, M., *Tokyo City Guide*, Ryuko Tsushin Co. Ltd, Tokyo, 1984

Committee for Economic Development of Australia, *Labour–Management Relations Australia and Japan*, Keizai Doyukai and CEDA, Sydney, 1989

DeVrye, C., *Good Service is Good Business*, Prentice-Hall, Sydney, 1993

Hartzenbusch, N. and Shabecoff, *A Parents' Guide to Tokyo*, Shufuntomo, Tokyo, 1984

McQueen, I., *Japan—A Travel Survival Kit,* Lonely Planet, Melbourne, 1986

Maloney, D., *Japan—It's Not All Raw Fish*, Japan Times, Tokyo, 1984

Morita, A., *Made in Japan*, Collins, UK, 1987

Nagasawa, K. and Condon C., *Eating Cheap in Japan*, Shufunotomo, Tokyo, 1985

National Police Agency, *Rules of the Road*, Japan Automobile Federation,
Tokyo, 1979

Nevins, T., *Labour Pains and the Gaijin Boss*, Japan Times, Tokyo, 1984

Okada, R., *Japanese Proverbs and Proverbial Phrases,* Japan Travel Bureau,
Tokyo, 1955

Pascale, R.T. and Athos, A.G., *The Art of Japanese Management*, Penguin,
UK, 1987

Reischauer, E., *Japan—The Story of a Nation*, Tuttle, Tokyo, 1981

Rogers, E., *Staying Healthy in Japan*, Tokyo Weekender, Japan, 1985

Rowland, D., *Japanese Business Etiquette*, Warner Brothers, New York, 1985

Sumitomo Corporation, *Aspects of Japanese Culture, Tradition and Behaviour*,
Tokyo, 1982

Saisho, Y., *How I Succeeded in Business in a Male-Dominated Society. Women
Executives in Japan*, Yuri, Tokyo, 1981

Illustrated 'Salaryman' in Japan, Japan Travel Bureau Inc., 1987

Turrent, J., *Around Tokyo. Vol. 2*, The Japan Times, Tokyo, 1984

Whiting, R., *You Gotta Have Wa*, Vintage Books, New York, 1989

The World Fellowship Committee of the Young Women's Christian
Association of Tokyo, Japan, *Japanese Etiquette. An Introduction*, Tuttle,
Tokyo, 1985